Training Your Dachshund

Amy Fernandez

BARRON'S

About the Author

Amy Fernandez is an award-winning author, painter, and illustrator. Amy has been a breeder of champion dogs since 1980. She has written several articles and books on dog care and training, and is the president of the Dog Writers Association of America.

Photo Credits

Kent Dannen: pages 4, 12 (top), 17, 18, 22, 23, 40, 41, 54, 55, 57, 61, 63, 84, 106, 118, 119, 121, 127, 129, 136, 137, 138, and 141; Tara Darling: pages 81, 86, 96, 113, 123 (bottom), and 130; Cheryl Ertelt: pages 3, 73 (bottom right), 89, 93, 99, 143, and 152; Jean Fogle: 21, 31, 67, 68, 79, 101, and 120; Isabelle Francais (Pet Profiles): pages 6, 12 (middle and bottom), 27, 49, 65, 66, 71, 73 (top left), 74, 76, 83, 104, 107, 108, 117, 122, 123 (top), and 131; Pets by Paulette: pages 2, 8 (top and bottom), 10, 11, 14, 28, 33, 37, 43, 44, 45, 46, 47 (top and bottom), 48, 53, 73, 98, 102, 134, 144, 146, 147, 149, and 150.

Acknowledgments

This book could not have been written without the Dachshund experts who generously shared their knowledge: Edith Colaneri, Robin Gianopolus, Michele, Kepalas, and the world's greatest dog trainer, Debbie Feliziani.

Thank you to my wonderful, patient, talented editor, Anne McNamara.

Cover Credits

Front cover: Pets by Paulette; back cover, inside front cover, inside back cover: Isabelle Francais.

All inquiries should be addressed to:
Barron's Educational Series, Inc.
250 Wireless Boulevard
Hauppauge, NY 11788
www.barronseduc.com

ISBN-13: 978-0-7641-3983-3
ISBN-10: 0-7641-3983-5

Library of Congress Catalog Card No. 2008000286

Library of Congress Cataloging-in-Publication Data
Fernandez, Amy.
   Training your dachshund / Amy Fernandez.
      p. cm.
   ISBN-13: 978-0-7641-3983-3
   ISBN-10: 0-7641-3983-5
   1. Dachshunds. I. Title.

SF429.D25F47 2008
636.753'8—dc22   2008000286

Printed in China
9 8 7 6 5 4 3 2 1

Important Note

This book tells the reader how to train a Dachshund. The author and the publisher consider it important to point out that the advice given in the book is meant primarily for dogs of excellent physical health and good character.

Anyone who adopts a fully grown dog should be aware that the animal has already formed its basic impressions of human beings. There are dogs that as a result of bad experiences with humans behave in an unnatural manner or may even bite. Only people that have experience with dogs should take in such an animal.

Even well-behaved and carefully supervised dogs sometimes do damage to someone else's property or cause accidents. It is, therefore, in the owner's interest to be adequately insured against such eventualities, and we strongly urge all dog owners to purchase a liability policy that covers their dog.

Contents

1 *The Versatile Dachshund*

Dachshunds have remained one of the most popular breeds since anyone began keeping records of such things. According to a recent AKC survey, Dachshunds rank among the top ten breeds in 39 of 50 major cities in the United States. A popular sporting dog in many parts of Europe since the 1700s, they were an instant hit at the early dog shows of the 1860s. This in turn, ignited the demand for Dachshunds as pets. Though everyone at the time seemed to love Dachshunds, none were able to agree on their purpose. The breed proved to be equally appealing as show dogs, pets, and hunters. This amazing versatility has not only guaranteed the Dachshund's continuing status, it provides insights into the baffling complexities of Dachshund temperament.

Dachshund Personality

Ask a group of Dachshund lovers to describe their pets' personalities and you may wonder if they are discussing the same breed! Dachshunds are devoted, independent, adventurous, cautious, stubborn, biddable, staid, comical, introverted, extroverted, and everything in between. A

breed's original purpose is usually an accurate indicator of temperament, and history confirms that the Dachshund was first and foremost a hunting dog. Later it became celebrated as a companion and show dog.

Even in this capacity, the dog's function was characterized by versatility rather than specialization. Dachshunds were considered all-purpose sporting dogs and trained successfully for almost every facet of hunting. In addition to their undeniable credentials as earthdogs (dogs that follow their game into tunnels or dens dug in the ground), they were used to track wounded animals, and flush game out of cover. Their talents were not limited to small game. German sportsmen were well acquainted with the Dachshund's prowess as a boar hunter. According to nineteenth-century breeder/judge Enoch Hutton, "In covert shooting they are equal to any Spaniel, and far superior when it is close and thick. They can be broken to quarter ground and work game to the gun and taught to retrieve, they do not tire easily and will follow their chase for many hours without a break, a ten or twelve mile run seeming good fun to them. In temper they are somewhat stubborn, and require great patience in breaking, but when once trained their great intelligence leaves

Dachshunds are equally happy to sit on the settee...

nothing to be desired by the sportsman who admires the breed." (*The Illustrated Book of the Dog*, by Vero Shaw, 1881)

Breed Heritage

Although the Dachshund is most closely associated with Germany, many historians contend that the breed originated in France, descending from the Basset Hound. It is believed that both breeds shared a common ancestor in the now extinct St. Hubert Hound, one of the five principal hunting breeds of medieval Europe. It is also quite likely that an array of regional breeds were incorporated into the Dachshund gene pool as the breed took shape over the centuries.

The Dachshund's existence in Germany can be traced back a little over 200 years. By the nineteenth century, as many as twelve varieties of Dachshunds had been developed in Germany for various types of sport. The major divisions were the *Geradbeinige* Dachshund, a taller straight-legged dog used for hunting above ground, and the *Krummbeinige* Dachshund, a crooked-legged, smaller type used for routing fox and badger from underground dens.

Half a century later it became customary to further divide these varieties according to their smooth, wire, and long-haired coats. The smooth Dachshund was the first variety to become widely popular, but *The Dachshund Handbook* by Clifford Hubbard (1950) cites several natural history sources that mention the existence of three coat types in Germany in the 1700s. In his authoritative reference work *A History and Description of the Modern Dogs of Great Britain and Ireland* (1893), historian Rawdon Lee states that the German Teckel-Klub, founded in 1888, recognized three varieties of Dachshund: smooth-haired, rough-haired, and long-haired.

As Dachshunds became prevalent in England, breeders began to further divide them according to weight, color, and height.

These well-meaning efforts to rigidly categorize the breed failed to address the Dachshund's versatility or eclectic ancestry, and ultimately intensified confusion about the breed's form, function, and inherent nature.

...and to explore the great outdoors.

When Dachshunds first came to the attention of kennel clubs in England and America they were known as German Badger Hounds, a name that endured long after the breed was officially recognized. According to some canine historians the Dachshund's ultimate designation as a hound was simply due to an error of translation. Badger (*dachs*) dog (*hund*) was erroneously translated as badger hound. As James Watson explains in *The Dog Book* (1907), "The meaning of the word 'hund' not being so well known as it should have been in England, led to the breed being

The Dachshund Field Trial Club of Germany held its first meeting a few miles outside of Berlin on April 6 of 1881. This predated the formation of the German breed club by seven years, supporting the notion that the Dachshund was primarily perceived as a working dog in its native land.

given a class in the studbook under the title of Dachshunds (or German Badger Hounds), in place of 'badger dogs,' and this led to their being considered hounds and bred for hound heads, in place of the correct terrier type."

Because of the Dachshund's unrivaled skill as an earth dog, many considered it a terrier rather than a hound. Dachshunds unquestionably possessed the resolve and courage equal to any working terrier and excelled at traditional terrier jobs of drawing and driving fox and badger.

In reality, it is difficult to designate them as either a hound or a terrier based on their ancestry, form, function, or temperament. It's fair to say that Dachshund temperament includes a mixture of both hound and terrier traits. After two hundred years this debate continues. Fédération Cynologique Internationale (FCI) countries have resolved this dilemma by classifying Dachshunds as a separate group of breeds.

Innate Temperament

Consistently reproducing specialized personality traits remains one of the mysteries of dog breeding. In the 1930s, researcher Leon Whitney conducted hundreds of test breedings to identify specific genes controlling behaviors such as pointing, retrieving, trail barking, liveliness, and even the propensity to smile. It was obvious that many of these were inherited, but their blueprint proved nearly impossible to decipher.

In part, this is because behavior is produced by complex genetic factors and variable combinations of learning and instinct. Throughout the animal world, countless actions are initiated and governed by instinct—behavior patterns pre-programmed into an animal's nervous system. They ensure that appropriate responses to complicated, sometimes life-threatening, situations are instantly available to every member of the species—regardless of experience or judgment. The disadvantage is that these automatic responses are inflexible, and not always appropriate. True instincts are reflexive and cannot be modified by learning.

The ability to override instinct varies drastically between species. Dogs have an extremely well developed ability to do this. Many canine behaviors once believed to be completely governed by instinct are now recognized as a combination of instinct and learning. In terms of survival, this provides a tremendous advantage. In

Miniatures: Red smooth, black and tan longhair, red wirehair.

Canine Drives

- *Defensive or fight drive is the overriding desire to avoid danger and ensure self-preservation. This response is basic to species survival. Depending on the nature of the threat and a dog's temperament, a defensive response can elicit fight or flight strategies.*
- *Social or pack drive is the inherent need to be accepted as part of a social group. It's expressed as a desire for social interaction and produces the dog's instinctive need for social order and understanding of pack hierarchy.*
- *Prey or play drive is the desire to hunt for food. It encompasses a range of behaviors associated with locating prey, hunting, and eating. The common denominator is that all the associated actions are self-rewarding.*

would be more accurate to say that they energize certain behaviors, rather than control them. Their role is to motivate responses that are most relevant to a dog's survival at any given time. Canine behaviorists refer to these instinctive motivations as drives.

Drives can be stimulated by internal and external factors. For instance, extreme hunger will stimulate prey drive, the arrival of a beloved companion will elicit social drive, and a sudden threat will trigger defensive drive. Instinctive behaviors are genetically programmed to emerge automatically as puppies mature. In general, they will become more pronounced and will not diminish with age.

Breed Specific Tendencies

Structural and chemical anatomy share equal responsibility for the unique traits that define each breed. Biological deter-

contrast to many other species (including the dog's immediate predecessor, the wolf), dogs easily utilize a choice of strategies to confront the challenges of their environment.

The dog's instinctively based behaviors are ancestral survival skills, coloring perception in a way comparable to human emotions. Emotional responses ensure that we remain sensitive to many aspects of our environment. They can also skew our perception or spur us to impetuous actions. Canine emotions stem from the survival needs to hunt, to belong to a social pack, and to stave off threats. It

Standard Dachshunds generally weigh between 16 and 32 pounds. Miniatures should not exceed 11 pounds in weight.

Puppies have an innate drive to socialize. Their earliest social interaction takes place with littermates. This need is later transferred to human family members.

miners control every aspect of a dog's development from size, to coat, to the chemical structure of neurotransmitters influencing behavior. Specialized differences in temperament and working ability run much deeper than training; they are based in specific neurological patterns. For example, low levels of dopamine production will produce a lethargic temperament, while high levels will cause hyperactivity.

Hunting Instinct and Prey Drive

Since the Dachshund was bred to be a hunter, prey drive tends to be well represented in the breed's personality. But for most Dachshunds, full-time hunting has been replaced by a life as a companion or a participant in dog sports. That doesn't mean these skills have disappeared or that they are going to waste.

The mindset induced by prey drive ensures that all sensory information—smells, sights, and sounds—are efficiently utilized to hunt. Cliché manifestations of predatory behavior include stalking, chasing, and sometimes killing other animals. These are the most obvious representations of prey drive, but far from the only ones. It encompasses any activity associated with investigating the environment, locating prey, or eating. This can motivate a tremendous variety of behaviors such as intently watching movements at a distance, sniffing the ground, excited barking, chasing, jumping, digging, and seizing, shaking, or burying objects. In the case of Dachshunds, prey behavior usually comprises a mixture of terrier's instinct to stalk and kill vermin and the hound's inclination to track and course prey.

Prey drive is fairly easy to interpret when the target is actual prey, but these behaviors are rarely confined to that narrow setting and the urge to hunt is not always motivated by hunger. Many forms of playing are motivated by prey drive. These activities may be directed towards human or canine playmates, toys, pants legs, blankets, dishtowels, or other animals. Regardless of whether they involve hunting or playing, the activities associated with prey drive have some common features. They are characterized by an attentive, playful attitude, and gestures such as a wagging tail held slightly high, alert ears, and high-pitched friendly barking.

Instinct and Training

Differences in sensory patterns and innate responses have a substantial impact on the ability to comprehend and respond to specific types of training. Before you begin training your Dachshund it is imperative to understand the breed's character and the reasons why innate temperament contribute to functionality. Recognizing the Dachshund's specific abilities helps to accomplish training objectives.

- *It helps you to predict your dog's responses in various training situations.*
- *It keeps your training expectations within a reasonable framework based on the breed's instinctive behaviors.*
- *It allows you to modify your training techniques to take advantage of the breed's natural talents.*

Some Dachshunds possess very little prey drive while others seem born to the life of a hunter. Observe your dog's reactions during play. Dogs with strong prey drive are tremendously interested in toys and games and tend to be very alert to changes in their environment. They cannot resist chasing a moving target, and may become completely unresponsive to you when this urge takes over. This desire to chase, grab, and shake toys, or play tug of war are all motivated by prey drive and can emerge as early as six weeks of age.

Prey behavior is self-rewarding, which explains why it can strongly influence so many aspects of temperament.

- lowers stress
- relieves anxiety
- encourages focused attention

Assessing Personality

Behavioral drives influence how a dog will react to a particular situation, but these responses are not pre-programmed. Dogs typically exhibit a variety of responses to similar situations. Personality is the combined result of genetically predetermined (physical and biochemical) and acquired characteristics. Behavioral traits never exist in isolation; they are continually influenced by other aspects of temperament. Your Dachshund's motivations may seem obvious, but the personality traits responsible for them are blended together in a highly individual manner.

Balanced Temperament

Ideally, all aspects of your Dachshund's personality should be balanced, resulting in a temperament that is focused, motivated, and under control. Balanced temperament reflects all the normal Dachshund instincts but remains moderate, flexible, and adaptable. This is the end product of good genes and capable training.

Normal Parameters of Dachshund Temperament

Dachshund temperament reflects a blend of terrier spunk and tenacity with houndy independence and sensitivity. This remark-

Puppies hone their hunting skills through mock fights with canine playmates.

able combination has been responsible for the breed's versatility as a sporting dog. It also explains why Dachshunds may not respond predictably in conventional training situations. Play-it-safe responses don't provide any advantage to the working Dachshund.

A good earthdog must be able to revise every game plan as necessary and continue pursuing a goal despite obstacles and adversity. Absolute fearlessness is essential when confronting aggressive quarry in the confines of a dark tunnel. These traits maximize the chance of success and minimize the effort required to train or motivate the dog.

The American Kennel Club Dachshund standard describes temperament this way: *"the Dachshund is clever, lively, and courageous to the point of rashness, persevering in above and below ground work, with all the senses well-developed. Any display of shyness is a serious fault."*

Puppies can express their instinctive prey drive in some unusual ways.

Training Tip

Ideally, temperament evaluation should take place within the context of breed specific tendencies while remaining mindful of typical personality variations of the breed. The results will provide far better insights into evolving behavior patterns such as self-assurance, independence, stress tolerance, and sensitivity. Erratic responses can also reveal an unbalanced personality in the making.

- Calmness and confidence are good indications of a balanced temperament. Puppies can rarely be described as calm but it is still possible to assess this trait in a young pup. Pick up the pup in one hand and hold it supporting the chest and allowing the legs to hang down. A calm pup will remain relaxed. A nervous pup will become tense and wrap its legs tightly around your arm and may commence shaking and whining. An overly excitable pup will continuously wriggle, squirm, and fight to get down.
- A good Dachshund must possess the confidence to fearlessly confront quarry. It's possible to get a glimpse of this trait in young pups by observing their reactions when faced with something startling or unfamiliar. An unexpected loud noise will usually stop them in their tracks. The brave pup will immediately recover and continue what it was doing.

A timid pup will run for cover and require much more recovery time. An excitable pup may commence running about frantically and barking. Their reaction to an unfamiliar location is equally telling. A confident pup may seem initially confused by new surroundings but soon begins exploring the territory. A timid pup may cower and refuse to budge. An excitable pup will become agitated, hyperactive, and eventually exhausted in response to the novel situation.

- A puppy's immediate ancestors also provide priceless information about temperament. A puppy's mother contributes much more than her genes to her offspring's personality. Her temperament and behavior exert a tremendous influence on neurological development both before and after their birth. Most importantly, she exerts a tremendous educational impact on her pups, as long as she has the opportunity to remain with them during their weaning period. The dam's personality will provide the most accurate information about a puppy's future behavior, but she is not the only source of information. The prevailing temperament traits of all close relatives will also provide invaluable clues. Are they busy, quiet, noisy, aloof, gentle, demanding? Chances are the pups will share the same.

However, a dog behaving this way in response to formal training might be described as stubborn or mischievous and might even be labeled as incorrigible or neurotic.

The Dachshund breed standard also calls for well-developed senses. A willing hunter must utilize all senses in the quest for prey. This means constantly scanning the environment for telltale movement,

If your puppy has a natural instinct to retrieve, encourage it.

Even more amazing is their sense of smell. Dogs have 220 million olfactory receptors compared to a human's paltry five million. Not only can they detect incredibly minute odor traces, they can differentiate various scents by separating and analyzing odor molecules, much as we would study the musical notes of a symphony.

In addition to senses equipped to detect and process huge amounts of environmental information, Dachshund brains are hardwired to process it in ways that are meaningless from a human perspective. A highly motivated Dachshund utilizing these skills in a training class might be labeled as disinterested, distracted, or learning impaired.

It's also imperative for a working Dachshund to bond effortlessly with humans. A hunting dog that refused to relinquish its catch or failed to return home after the hunt would be useless. The motivation to do this requires sensitivity to human social dynamics along with the basic need for contact and acceptance. Dachshunds are extremely attuned to human reactions and possess an uncanny ability to interpret subtle human gestures. This makes it easy for them to bond with their owners, but can complicate training. Never assume that you can hide your emotions from your Dachshund. A bad attitude on your part can create an avoidance response toward training as easily as harsh treatment.

sniffing the air and ground for scent, and listening for faint sounds above and below. These skills cannot be taught. They are the product of strong prey drive and finely tuned senses. A Dachshund's sensory capacity is impressive to say the least. They possess a wide field of vision, excellent night vision, and acute sensitivity to motion. Many hunting dogs can spot a moving object half a mile away. They lack full color vision but they don't need it in order to hunt successfully.

Dachshunds can hear frequencies far lower and higher than those perceptible to the human ear. The mobility of their ears also equips them with precise sound localization ability. They can detect sounds at four times the range of human hearing and pinpoint the source quickly and accurately.

Temperament Testing

Formalized temperament tests first came into general use as means of assessing prospective candidates for specialized training such as military or guide dog work.

A puppy's temperament remains a work in progress until adulthood.

Because these dogs required lengthy complex training, puppies needed to possess a particular set of personality traits and promising candidates had to be selected at a relatively young age. They were specifically bred and raised with this goal in mind; therefore standardized testing could be used to reliably evaluate aptitude.

Controversy has arisen concerning its value outside a controlled setting because of the numerous variables that can complicate the results. Puppies come from a wide range of environmental and genetic backgrounds and face a variety of lifestyles as pets. Under these circumstances, it is tricky to make clear determinations about character or predict potential success in an unknown lifestyle. Many temperament traits do not emerge

until adolescence or stabilize until adulthood. A balanced temperament is a combination of genetics, socialization, and training. The success of the canine species is rooted in its ability to adapt. However, each dog's personal strategies vary tremendously. Behavior is never static and emotional reactions can take many forms.

Many aspects of a dog's temperament can change over time and responses don't always remain consistent. For instance, one sufficiently noteworthy experience can completely revise an impressionable puppy's personality. It's also true that puppies have good and bad days just like the rest of us. It's safe to say that the results of temperament tests are valid at the time of testing, under those specific conditions.

Temperament Stereotypes

■ *Smooth Dachshunds were believed to be more aloof and predatory in nature, a trait attributed to their crossbreeding to Bloodhounds, Basset Hounds, and Foxhounds. This theory has since been discredited.*

■ *Wirehaired Dachshunds were described as more tenacious, bold, and resilient in nature, thanks to crossbreeding with Wirehaired Pinschers, Dandie Dinmonts, Scottish Terriers, and Skye Terriers.*

■ *Longhaired Dachshunds were described as more sociable and even tempered. A Spaniel cross has been discounted by Dachshund authorities but crossbreeding to other longhaired sporting breeds has not been ruled out.*

By 1900, the miniature Dachshund, then known as the Rabbit Teckel, was well established in Germany and in 1905 the Kaninchen-teckel Klub was formed to promote them. Like their larger counterparts they were primarily hunting dogs, used in place of ferrets to drive out small burrowing game. Although miniature Dachshunds occurred naturally, canine reference books from the nineteenth-century reveal that breeders customarily crossbred them with established toy dogs to further reduce size. This would help to explain descriptions of them as more affectionate and sensitive.

Top: Smooth Dachshund
Middle: Wirehair Dachshund
Bottom: Longhair Dachshunds

This does not imply that Dachshund temperament develops randomly. Normal variations of personality will remain within certain boundaries. Although they offer no guarantees temperament tests can help to evaluate and record personality development. It provides insight into the probabilities of future behavior, but can never predict future behavior or the appearance of undesirable traits.

All dogs share certain inherent traits even though their expression is modified through selective breeding, environment, and individual genetic make up. That explains why such a range of personalities exists in every breed—dominant, submissive, sociable, calm, and sensitive, all fall within the parameters of normal behavior.

Subjectivity also plays a role in our perceptions of canine behavior. Impartiality is essential but it can be difficult to avoid broad-brush interpretations or overly optimistic assessments, both of which can obscure the true picture.

Temperamental Differences Between the Varieties

Most modern breeds, including Dachshunds, are products of crossbreeding between established types within the last hundred years. The Dachshund is a blend of German, French, and English hounds, terriers, and sporting breeds. All varieties include some crossbreeding in their backgrounds. As such, dogs of similar breeding can possess mixtures of character traits reflecting variable ancestry. Hybridized behaviors may appear alike superficially but their genetic basis may be encoded completely differently, leading to a range of variable responses. This is another factor that helps to explain the idiosyncrasies of Dachshund temperament.

Dachshund temperament has stabilized considerably since these experiments took place. Extreme traits such as the savagery described in nineteenth-century Dachshunds have been eliminated. In the twentieth century, crossbreeding has been replaced by interbreeding between the varieties. This also accounts for the many similarities and nuances of temperament common to all Dachshund varieties.

A pup's reaction when picked up and restrained will tell you a lot about temperament.

13

2 Are You a Dachshund Person?

Centuries of anecdotal evidence suggest a mysterious connection between talent, intelligence, sensitivity, and a great appreciation for Dachshunds. The breed's admirers have included Queen Victoria, Pablo Picasso, David Hockney, Andy Warhol, Noel Coward, Marlon Brando, Napoleon, Jacques Cousteau, Joan Crawford, Henry James, P.G. Wodehouse, Vincent Price, Madonna, Brooke Astor, Fay Wray, James Dean, and Errol Flynn, to name a few. In the past 150 years, the Dachshund's multi-faceted charms have catapulted the breed to iconic status. The reasons for this are understandable. With two sizes, three coats, and countless colors there is a Dachshund to suit every taste. Even the largest Dachshund is portable and easily managed in an urban environment. Grooming requirements are modest, as the dogs shed little and emit no doggy odor. They are energetic and sturdy with a "big-dog" personality, but don't require the space and physical endurance needed to manage larger dogs. They acclimate well to multi-dog households and make excellent watchdogs despite their compact size. Beautiful, loyal, playful, affectionate, and a bit quirky, their status is well earned.

The Wrong Reasons to Get a Dachshund

With so much to recommend it, this breed really doesn't need a sales manager—or maybe it does. Because Dachshunds are so

Dapple and piebald Dachshunds look quite attractive, but they are more prone to sight and hearing problems.

popular, they are relatively easy to find. This provides an ongoing temptation to acquire one for the wrong reason. If you suddenly develop the notion to have a Dachshund, this can be accomplished with an e-mail, phone call, or trip to the local pet shop. Superficially this may seem like a harmless way to enhance your life. The media has done a great deal to encourage romanticized perceptions of dog owner-ship and these blind dates work out okay often enough. Unfortunately, it also explains how many unhappy dog/owner relationships begin. Despite access to a wealth of information, many potential owners continue to make this important decision without adequate research or forethought.

A large share of the breed's negative publicity stems from health or tempera-ment problems traceable to irresponsible breeding. Research studies regularly con-firm the familiar reasons why dogs are surrendered to rescue groups and shelters. Most often, owners are unprepared to deal with the responsibilities of keeping a dog. They either lack the physical ability, time, living space, and financial resources or have unrealistic expectations of what dog ownership entails. Many novice own-ers find themselves unable to cope with the demands of training a puppy or suc-cessfully introducing a new dog to other members of their household. Health prob-lems also account for a fair proportion of shelter surrenders. Needless to say, these issues are far less likely to occur when pur-chasing a Dachshund from a responsible breeder.

Of course, any Dachshund can develop problems if forced to adapt to an unten-

Top Ten Reasons Why Dogs Are Surrendered to Public Shelters
1. Moving
2. "No pet" clause in lease
3. Too many pets in household
4. Expenses of caring for the dog
5. Personal problems
6. Inadequate facilities to keep the dog
7. Cannot find homes for puppies
8. Lack of time to care for the dog
9. Dog's illness
10. Biting
Source: Canine and Feline Theriogenology, Johnston, Kustritz, Olson, 2001

able environment. If you are seeking a sta-tus symbol or surrogate child, look else-where. No matter how well bred or well trained, dogs retain an unfailing tendency to act like dogs! Puppies have accidents until they are housetrained. Without ade-quate supervision they chew, bark, dig holes, and tip over trashcans. Puppies require a bigger commitment than fully grown dogs, but don't assume that adults are problem free or self-sufficient. Before you even consider adding a Dachshund to your life take an honest look at the breed's socialization, training, and care require-ments. Appreciating a dog and living with a dog are two entirely different things. In addition to being attracted to a Dachs-hund's appearance and manner, you must be equally attracted to the breed's inher-ent nature. Although every dog is a unique individual, a good portion of Dachshund behavior is a predictable result of its genetic heritage.

Dogs have devoted 12,000 years to figuring out how to coexist with us. Their overwhelming success is a testament to their proficiency. Our faith in their adaptability has also unfortunately led to unreasonable expectations about what they can and should do. Every dog has certain essential requirements as well as finite limits to coping skills.

This is not the breed for you if you don't like surprises. Understanding Dachshund character makes it far easier to anticipate training challenges and address behavior issues as they occur. This is one of the reasons why Dachshunds require a great deal of personal attention. If you know what to expect, you are far more likely to get a grip on the ongoing parade of unforeseen situations before it gets out of hand. If not, you may eventually face an unhappy choice of giving up your dog or completely revising your life to cope with chronic misbehavior.

You also need to consider the logistics.

- Dachshunds don't shed heavily but they will leave hair on carpets and furniture and can track in an impressive amount of mud on a rainy day. This can add up to a lot of extra cleaning, especially if you share a small living space with your pet.
- Your Dachshund will need an accessible retreat. This could be part of your kitchen or bedroom, or a crate. Few people have the luxury of devoting 24/7 to their dog to ensure adequate supervision. Most Dachshunds require either supervision or a managed environment to ensure their safety.
- Dogs can and do adapt to spending time alone but they are a social species,

and crave interaction. You should not expect a dog to accept being left alone or crated unless trained to do so. In the case of Dachshunds, chronic barking or home destruction may result.

- Confinement is not a suitable substitute for training. Be prepared to devote necessary time and effort to helping your Dachshund learn your household rules and adapt to your personal routine. Family members may (or may not) pitch in and help. You can also hire a dog walker or daycare service but you must be prepared to take ultimate responsibility.
- All dogs need regular exercise even though their actual demands vary drastically ranging from 15 minutes to two or three hours per day. This is not easy to estimate based on size or body type; to a great extent, the amount of activity a dog needs is biochemically determined. A Dachshund should have at least 30 to 60 minutes of outdoor exercise daily. Even though Miniature Dachshunds may get sufficient exercise running around the house they still need daily outings for socialization, recreation, and mental stimulation.

In addition to the potential complications just mentioned, you should also be prepared for the costs. Regardless of whether you purchase a puppy from a breeder or adopt from a shelter or rescue group, ongoing dog care is part of the deal. Plan to spend at least $500 to $1,000 per year for food, veterinary care, and supplies.

As a rule, advance planning is the best way to keep costs manageable. For instance, a poorly bred pet shop puppy purchased impetuously will cost more than a puppy acquired from a responsible

Miniature Dachshunds out for their daily romp.

breeder. Because the parents of commercially produced puppies are not screened for genetic health disorders, pet shop puppies are also more liable to experience immediate or late onset health disorders—both of which are notoriously expensive. In contrast, a puppy from a breeder may

Veterinary Behaviorists

Increasing numbers of dog owners seek professional assistance to cope with unmanageable behavior simply because they are unprepared for the realities of dog ownership. A canine behavioral therapist specializes in diagnosing and treating complex behavior issues that don't readily respond to conventional training methods. According to the American Veterinary Medical Association, board-certified veterinary behaviorist is among the fastest growing specialized fields within the profession.

cost half as much but finding one will require twice the time and effort on your part. Veterinary expenses will likely be limited to routine care. Training will also be less complicated because the puppy will have had an introduction to socialization and training prior to placement. Responsible breeders rarely place puppies before twelve weeks of age. Ongoing contact with their dam during these weeks is crucial to their social development. It ensures that they learn social skills that will impact their future ability to interact with both dogs and humans.

Pet shop puppies are normally sent to a wholesaler at seven weeks of age and offered for retail sale at eight weeks. This schedule severely limits a puppy's opportunities to interact with other dogs and learn social skills before trying to assimilate into a pack. This is further complicated by the fact that the puppy must adjust to living with a different species.

Puppies learn basic social skills by playing with littermates.

Pet insurance can help defray the expense of vet care although many insurance plans do not always cover treatments for genetically based disorders or consultations with a veterinary behaviorist. Behavioral problems can max out your credit cards in the blink of an eye. Consultation and treatment with a certified veterinary behaviorist can run several thousand dollars. But it could be worse. Misbehaving dogs have been the cause of evictions, lawsuits, and skyrocketing homeowner's insurance premiums.

Pricey Pets

Annual dog ownership expenses according to the American Pet Products Manufacturers Association's (APPMA) 2005-2006 National Pet Owners Survey

Routine vet care $211
Unexpected vet care $574
Food $241
Grooming products $107
Vitamins $123
Treats $68
Toys $45

Your Expectations About Dog Training

An ongoing commitment to your Dachshund's training is the easiest way to prevent behavior problems. Some owners avoid training because they anticipate months of repetitive work, but short, effective lessons can yield surprising results. In most cases, the socialization, housetraining, and constant supervision associated with raising a puppy are the most labor-intensive aspects of training. When they reach adulthood most Dachshunds become fairly undemanding. However, there are exceptions to this rule.

Your expertise as a trainer also feeds into the equation. Mastering skills such as effective communication and good timing take quite a bit longer for a novice owner than for one with previous dog-training experience. Some trainers have an inborn knack for properly timing commands and rewards. Others must develop this ability through practice.

Patience and consistency are essential. Whether you are dealing with a major or minor training issue, daily work to revise the problem is the only way to encourage the dog's behavior in the right direction. Major training problems won't be resolved overnight, but you can be certain that they won't get better by ignoring them.

Working with your Dachshund every day keeps you mindful of evolving behavior patterns, both good and bad. Unless you are paying attention, undesirable behavior may not receive the intervention it merits. Many problems can be easily managed if they are addressed early. For instance, wariness or shyness can eventually progress to growling, snapping, or biting. At that point, remedying the problem may require long-term behavior modification. At an earlier stage, socialization and training could have turned it around.

Maintaining a consistent routine is one of the easiest ways to implement and reinforce good habits and prevent bad ones. Walking your dog at scheduled times reinforces housetraining for several reasons. For one, the dog doesn't get the opportunity to have an accident on the rug. That response becomes less likely to

> **Training Tip**
> The amount of time and effort required for training depends on the dog's personality and the complexity of what you are trying to teach. A calm, balanced dog will be able to focus and learn more quickly than an excitable or timid dog. A rescue dog needing remedial training or behavior modification may require much more time and effort than a young, untrained puppy.

occur every time it is prevented from happening. Likewise, consistently rewarding the desired behavior instills a preferable alternate habit. The actual walk becomes a reward for the dog. It also usually includes praise or a treat for mission accomplished during the course of the walk. From your Dachshund's point of view, the idea of a nice clean carpet is completely irrelevant.

It's often said that dogs want to please us. Much of what your Dachshund does may be pleasing but it's not inspired by any altruistic incentive to make you happy. This misguided belief has fostered the idea that dogs should be naturally well behaved due to some inherent understanding of human expectations. Dogs are adept at interpreting our social signals and exploiting their environment. That is not quite the same as wanting to follow our rules. If you do not provide boundaries or a structured routine your Dachshund will form habits based on feedback from the environment. Consciously or otherwise, you probably encourage certain behaviors in your dog.

How Dogs Learn

Formal and accidental learning never occurs randomly. Despite the technical names bestowed on them by scientists, these concepts are fairly obvious and apply to many species.

1. Operant conditioning. Dogs acquire a great deal of knowledge by systematically exploring and experimenting with their environment, forming good and bad associations based on what they discover. They constantly revise their behavior patterns according to what is working and what is not, regardless of whether you are involved in the process. "Live and learn" is the Dachshund mantra. Behaviorists have labeled this process operant conditioning. The dog easily grasps the cause and effect connection between an action and its immediate result. Learning often occurs after a single experience because the link is so obvious, powerful, and relevant to the dog's basic needs. It does not require much in the way of repeated effort to train a dog to beg at the table or sleep on the bed. Nothing compels the dog to make these choices but the behavior remains consistent because the dog instinctively enjoys that payoff. Other motivations are slightly more complicated. These rewards can include internal and environmental factors. Some of these are beyond our control and others completely escape our notice. For humans this might be emotional satisfaction of public approval. For dogs it might be the emotional satisfaction of chewing up a chair.

2. Classical conditioning produces a learned association between a neutral signal and something inherently valuable to the dog such as food. The famous example is Pavlov training dogs to salivate at the sound of a bell. The dogs learned to associate the ringing bell—something previously irrelevant to them—to the imminent arrival of food—something of tremendous importance. Timing is everything. The meaningless stimulus and the important one must be presented in closely timed intervals for the dog to successfully make this connection. We're all familiar with its use in dog training. Repeatedly rewarding a correct response leads the dog to associate spoken commands with particular actions. Rather than learning how to speak English, the dog is forming learned associations between something irrelevant and something gratifying. Like operant conditioning, dogs make millions of associations this way. For instance, they have no innate love for can openers or car keys. But they invariably learn to associate these items with things they value highly. Eventually, the sound of jangling keys will elicit the same jubilant reaction as a ride in the car or a walk in the park.

3. Instinctive learning. Dogs can be trained to perform innumerable complex tasks and it's sometimes difficult to determine how much of this ability is inherent, or the result of human influence. Long before behaviorists were invented, breeders realized that the work of dog training could be minimized by starting with a dog who instinctively wanted to guard the house, herd the sheep, or catch the rabbit. Conditioning the dog through repetition and reinforcement

was unnecessary despite the complexity of these jobs because they were reinforced by the dog's internal responses. These behaviors also remain very stable because they are rooted in survival instincts. Dogs of every shape, size, and heritage reliably perform the same hardwired behaviors without training. Today, very few dogs engage in their traditional work and a large percentage of training focuses discouraging instinctive behaviors like digging and chasing.

Dachshunds are smart and adaptable, but training cannot be relied on to transform every facet of behavior. This crucial fact sometimes receives less attention than it merits in a training program. Traits learned through operant or classical conditioning are far more easily altered than those resulting from instinctive learning.

The good news is that many aspects of training can be built on instinctive patterns. The effortless ability to learn behaviors tied to natural instinct is the basis of many forms of specialized training like detection and search-and-rescue work. Rather than trying to force your Dachshund to ignore his natural instincts, work on directing them. This tried-and-true method of building a strong foundation of enthusiasm for training can be utilized to encourage focus, manipulate or moderate behavior, curb unwanted habits, or help a dog overcome stress and fear. Because these responses are intensely pleasurable and self-reinforcing, it has the added benefit of fostering a positive attitude about the training process. For

A large portion of training focuses on discouraging instinctive behaviors like digging.

instance, the opportunity to engage in some form of self-rewarding prey/play behavior can be used as a tremendously alluring reward in addition to providing a great outlet for pent up energy.

Your Expectations About Dachshund Behavior

"Some day, if I ever get a chance, I shall write a book, or warning, on the character and temperament of the dachshund and why he can't be trained and shouldn't be. I would rather train a striped zebra to balance an Indian club than induce a dachshund to heed my slightest command." E.B. White

E.B White did not earn his fame as a dog trainer, but there is a valid reason why this remains one of the most commonly quoted descriptions of Dachshund training.

They may be small, but Dachshunds can be surprisingly athletic and energetic.

The Dachshund's appeal as a companion and working dog is based on the breed's fundamental versatility. They are mischievous, sweet, resilient, loyal, stubborn, and distracted for precisely the same reasons. This is a package deal. On the other hand, the character of the breed is no excuse to overlook or accept bad habits. There is a critical difference between inherent breed traits and aberrant behavior. The Dachshund may not be a push-button breed, but that doesn't imply that training is impossible. Breeds that are motivated by their own initiative actually require a higher degree of training.

■ This includes consistent socialization to prevent puppies from becoming reserved towards strangers. This should be a part of training from the start of a puppy's first socialization period, which commences at approximately seven or eight weeks of age.

■ Dachshunds need an introduction to other species from a young age if you hope to suppress their predatory instinct toward cats, birds, or rodents. Make this a regular part of training from seven or eight weeks of age until adulthood.

■ Though they relish outdoor activities, off-lead exercise may never be a safe option for some Dachshunds. A dog must have rock-solid recall training before you even try this and many are never totally trustworthy off lead. Needless to say, this adds to your daily commitment of time and energy.

■ Leaving your Dachshund alone to exercise in a fenced yard is not an acceptable substitute for daily walks or interactive play. This is not an outdoor breed. Spending the day alone in a yard may seem fine from a human point of view but from the dog's standpoint it is no more appealing than confinement to a kennel. The dog has little motivation to exercise. The resulting boredom and anxiety instead lead to destructive chewing, digging, barking, or fence fighting.

■ Dachshunds tend to be a fairly active breed, both indoors and outdoors. Some Dachshunds calm down as they mature but others retain a high activity level indoors and outdoors throughout life. Adequate daily exercise and consistent training is a must if you want a well-behaved housedog.

■ A Dachshund's interest in social issues is low compared to breeds that instinctively seek social approval (such as Poodles and Golden Retrievers). While this trait does not make formal training simple, it is not a conscious decision to be difficult. Dachshunds were developed to work independently. Hunting a rat underground or tracking a wounded deer through the underbrush would be impossible it the dog had to constantly rely on humans for direction and encouragement.

■ Rather than acting out of habit, a Dachshund constantly evaluates the environment, makes new associations, and responds accordingly. Repetition may be the key to habit formation, but a Dachshund's behavior will always be influenced by competing motivations.

■ Intelligence and trainability are often defined as willingness and ability to quickly grasp ideas presented by a trainer. To a great extent, this is dependant on temperament and instinct. Regardless of actual intelligence, it will be difficult for a distracted dog to settle down and focus to absorb anything presented during training. Intelligence can also complicate the training process. The Dachshund's talent for forming quick associations also extends to learning bad habits and opportunistic behaviors. Intelligent dogs are also more apt to vary their responses and test their boundaries.

These are general examples of what to expect whether you are training your Dachshund for hunting, competitive sports, or simply to be a good companion. Success depends on your ability to recognize various aspects of temperament, understand their origin, and work with these natural tendencies.

Puppies use their mouths to explore their environment—another reason why good supervision is essential.

3 *Training Dogs vs. Training Dachshunds*

Despite their tremendous popularity, Dachshunds are often described as difficult to train. In large part, this perception is a result of predominant training theories of past decades. The Dachshund's contradictions of temperament rule out a cookie cutter approach. Trying to train a Dachshund through rigid repetition is pretty much guaranteed to fail. Successful Dachshund training utilizes an almost reverse approach. Your Dachshund is going to teach you how to train Dachshunds.

The Building Blocks of Training

Your Dachshund's motivations fall into three categories

- He wants to avoid things he doesn't like
- He will develop a habitual response
- He will satisfy himself

Training is not likely to be one of your Dachshund's top priorities. Rearranging this priority list is possible as long as you use psychology. If you've lived with this breed for even a short time, you probably discovered that simply telling a Dachshund to do something doesn't guarantee results.

Communication Skills

At times, this may be hard to believe, but you and your Dachshund are both striving to get on the same wavelength. This isn't due to any altruistic canine intention. Dogs are motivated to understand human communication because it is beneficial to them. They communicate with us in order to manipulate our actions in their favor.

Even though both parties are strongly motivated to get this project off the ground it is not always a 50/50 deal. At times, you will be doing a very large share of the work. Dogs speak many languages and each breed possesses slightly different sensory patterns. Some tune into human communication skills more easily, and they all interpret them a bit differently.

Successful communication is a cooperative act; it simply does not work without a sender and receiver. This sounds obvious but failing to pay attention to this concept underlies quite a few training problems. Messages may not be communicated effectively or may be misinterpreted, thereby eliciting an inappropriate response.

The next time your Dachshund begins barking uncontrollably, be aware of how you are interpreting that message as well as what you may be doing to reinforce it.

Dachshund as a Second Language

For training to be effective, you and your Dachshund must be on the same page.

You must be able to discern what kind of mood you are starting with before trying to manipulate your dog into a receptive mood. This may range from total boredom to acute anxiety, but you must elicit a calm, happy, and attentive attitude. This goes for you too. Communication is a two-way street. Don't try to conceal your emotional state from a Dachshund. They are experts in interpreting human behavior.

Using Vocal Tones to Convey Training Information

Hard as it may be to believe, your voice has limited value as a training tool. Make the most of it but use it effectively.

- Use an authoritative, neutral voice for commands.
- Use a soft, happy voice for praise.
- Use a low stern voice for corrections.
- Use a sweet, encouraging voice to reinforce behavior.
- Use an alert, clipped voice to create anticipation.

Consistent terminology is equally important. Use enough different words so your dog can clearly associate specific actions with certain words but don't overdo it. Keep your phrasing short and concise. Don't vary usage or add unnecessary words for emphasis. A continuous string of vocal corrections is an especially bad training habit. Just like humans, dogs become immune to nagging. Dachshunds long ago mastered the art of tuning out human communications.

Ritualized Communication

Dogs possess excellent ability to broadcast their desires and intentions, known as ritualized signals. From a survival standpoint, ritualized communication maximizes survival by preventing misunderstandings.

> **Training Tip**
>
> *Dogs often fool us into overestimating their ability to comprehend our spoken words. They respond with accuracy and sensitivity that belies their actual ability. Dogs communicate with each other through the use of olfactory signals, facial expressions, and body language. Despite this, they can be trained through classical conditioning to differentiate countless words. In large part they utilize other contextual clues such as unintentional body language, facial expressions, and vocal inflection. Avoid speaking in a monotone and consistently use specific tones to convey particular messages. It also helps to preface commands with an attention-getting command such as "Watch!" or "Look!"*

Home Schooling

Reinforcing Desired Behavior

Obedience trainers often remark that a Dachshund never makes the same mistake twice. In a sense that is true. If reprimanded for doing something wrong a Dachshund will very likely do it differently next time, but there is no guarantee you will like that any better. There are a million ways to do something wrong. Reprimanding your Dachshund for every mistake is time consuming, energy wasting, and guaranteed to create a negative attitude about training. Human and canine behaviorists agree that five positive reinforcements are needed to cancel out the impact of one reprimand. This is obviously an inefficient approach.

Your primary role as a trainer is to redirect your Dachshund's behavior by seeking actions to reward. This should become a regular feature of training even if your dog has a long way to go. Rather than ignoring every response that is not perfect, applaud any effort to get it right. Many a Dachshund habit results from interface with environment and they are naturally attuned to this process. Use the same principle by rewarding as much behavior as possible as long as it continues moving in the right direction.

For instance, stopping to glance back at you before dashing off after the squirrel in your backyard is not a textbook example of *come when called*, but it shows that the dog is still on your page and the response on the right track. Continually rewarding your dog's effort to shift out of predatory drive and calmly respond to you reinforces focus.

Even if you begin to suspect that your Dachshund is trying to outsmart you, resist the temptation to turn lessons into a battle of wits. Dachshunds are apt to experiment with many responses and continually gauge your reaction. This, rather than instant results or absolute obedience, is what you should expect from this breed. Putting yourself into the equation by providing feedback moves the training process along at a faster pace. Concentrate on encouraging the dog to make decisions voluntarily, while using mind games to stack the deck in favor of the choices you want. By reinforcing responsible behavior your Dachshund will eventually realize that self-control and cooperation consistently result in the best payoff. Here are a few useful exercises that will help make that happen.

Pay Attention

Getting a Dachshund to pay attention can be challenging but habit formation makes it much easier. Start by teaching your dog to make eye contact with you on command. This conditioned reflex comes in handy in countless Dachshund training situations. The importance of eye contact is sometimes overlooked when communicating with your dog. This breed is not built to instinctively look upwards but there is no other way to ensure your dog is paying you the slightest attention.

A gentle encouraging look can motivate a timid dog. A hard stare is a very effective reprimand. It can interrupt bad behavior and help you establish your alpha position in the relationship.

Start teaching this exercise in a quiet spot when the dog is fairly calm. Call the dog's name while holding treats in your left hand. As soon as the dog responds by making eye contact, attach a command such as "Look!" or "Watch!" and give the treat. Two or three seconds of eye contact is fine. You don't want the dog to become intimidated by misinterpreting prolonged staring as a hostile gesture. After approximately ten successful responses the dog will probably be unwilling to stop staring you in the eye.

When you feel that the dog is responding consistently, begin adding variations to the exercise. Try it when you are out for a walk or the dog is on the verge of veering off into prey drive. The more you do it the more ingrained the habit will become, making this a wonderful tool to divert your dog's attention on cue.

Getting your Dachshund's attention can be harder than you think. Use eye contact and hand signals to reinforce the idea.

Shaping

Because Dachshunds are hardwired to constantly evaluate, they need a lot of feedback. This general principle of dog training is known as shaping.

Shaping utilizes positive reinforcement such as food rewards, praise, or a clicker, to elicit a desired response. Slight approximations or small parts of the preferred behavior are systematically rewarded until they become shaped into the response you want to instill. Don't wait until the dog performs perfectly to offer a reward. Use every opportunity to provide feedback to encourage slow steady progress towards the goal. For example, if you give the *sit* command, and your Dachshund manages to get halfway into position, provide some feedback. This indicates that the dog is making a connection between the command and the action.

Shaping is an excellent motivator to encourage focused attention. Allowing the dog opportunities to size up the situation and choose a response is also a great confidence builder.

In contrast, forcing a Dachshund into the *sit* position or giving leash corrections for every incorrect response directly contradicts the breed's normal approach to problem solving. In short order, the dog will become frustrated or anxious, and start looking for an escape.

Targeting

Another useful technique in the Dachshund training tool box is targeting. Targeting

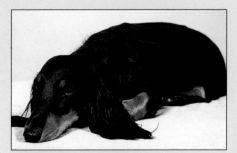

Teach your Dachshund to chill out by giving the relax command.

helps a dog learn to block out distractions and focus on specific goals. Dachshunds can cultivate this skill but it takes practice and sufficient incentive. Targeting is especially helpful for dogs that tend to be highly reactive or easily stressed. It's also a useful intermediary step to encourage apprehensive dogs to interact with people.

Target training rewards the dog for concentrating on a specific object on command. An easy way to start is by teaching your Dachshund to touch your hand on command. Hold your hand a couple of inches from the dog's nose with a treat ready in your other hand. Give the reward as soon as the dog's nose touches your hand for a sniff. Most dogs do this readily but if you encounter reluctance hold the treat in the target hand for a few seconds before transferring it to your reward hand. The scent will lure the dog to investigate your hand.

Repeat this until the dog makes the connection between touching nose to hand and getting a reward. When this link is established attach a verbal cue to the exercise and begin adding variables such as moving your hand farther away, switching hands, or transferring the command to an object. Targeting can be used to lure the dog's attention away from competing distractions or fearful situations. It's also an excellent quick fix in situations where it's necessary to de-escalate panic or overexcitement.

Relax

This exercise helps the dog learn to shift from agitated to calm state on command. Once the behavior is instilled, the state of mind will follow. Begin teaching this exercise indoors where there are few distractions. A bed or mat can help the dog make the desired association. Encourage the dog to sit or lie on the mat. At first, you may need to hold the dog's collar while you do this. As soon as you see any indication of relaxation in the dog's face or body such as a flickering eyelid or slowed breathing, give a command such as *relax*, and give a reward. Gently stroking the dog's ear or neck may help but some dogs find this too stimulating. Make sure your tone and body language are geared to encouraging relaxation. At first, two or three seconds may be as much as the dog can manage. If you have no success, ignore the dog for a minute or two and try again. Every Dachshund can master this exercise but natural temperament will play a big role in the process. Once the dog gets the idea, gradually add distractions and vary the locations where exercise is performed.

These techniques are useful tools to solve specific training problems. The more you use them the more you will cultivate your Dachshund's attention span and teach yourself to be more observant of your dog's shifting moods and behavior.

Hair-Raising Reasoning

Raised hackles evolved from the reflexive action of raising hairs to induce thermoregulation. Because of the biological connection between mental agitation and body temperature, this response also served as a barometer of underlying emotions. A dog that possessed the ability to control its own hackle-raising power enjoyed greater social advantage. Hair-raising displays thusly evolved from a purely biological function into a powerful ritualistic form of communication. Exaggeration enhanced the communication value of the message.

Like most canine behavior, ritualized gestures are a combination of innate and learned skills. Dogs cannot interpret or utilize them effectively unless they are learned and perfected via social interaction with other dogs.

Abbreviated Guide to Canine Gestures

Submissive
A submissive dog displays status and intentions through distinctive body language designed to convey small stature, including low body posture of crouching or crawling, head lowered, ears flattened back, tail tucked, gaze averted, often exaggerating this gesture by twisting the neck to the side. Accompanying anxiety may trigger physical reactions such as sweating paw pads, shedding, or dribbling urine. A submissive dog may also engage in appeasement rituals, such as whining, licking and nuzzling the dominant dog's mouth, or rolling over. These are typical behaviors of puppies. Wolves instinctively refrain from attacking pups, so the origin of this ritual is easy to understand.

Dominant
Typical dominance posture is meant to convey a stylized impression of extreme size and strength through a combination of high head carriage, arched neck, erect ears, and tail held high, with a rapid, stiff wag to advertise confidence and impending threat, accessorized with suitably low, rumbling vocal sounds.

Aggressive dominance incorporates raised hackles, bared teeth, and a menacing stare into this basic package. Slow deliberate movements are a typical precursor to aggression.

This may be accompanied by gestures such as standing over an opponent with front feet on the subordinate dog's back or closing the jaws around an opponent's muzzle, known as the muzzle pin. In other circumstances, these same gestures can typify play behavior, which reemphasizes the importance of putting these clues into appropriate context.

Vocal Tones
The canine vocal repertoire consists of whining, barking, and growling and easily employs the same sounds for many unrelated reasons. Even socially inept dogs are adept at vocal modulation. Whining and growling convey straightforward messages. High- and low-pitched sounds are easily interpreted by all dogs (and humans) in a range of situations.

Training Tip

It's critical to place every canine gesture into context when evaluating its meaning.

Some have multiple meanings. A direct stare is usually understood as an aggressive gesture, but dogs also stare when attempting to initiate play with dogs and humans. Other aspects of the dog's body language will reveal that no threat is implied. These are known as intention movements, gestures that indicate exactly what is on their mind.

Constantly sniffing the ground may indicate that the dog is intently seeking prey or may signal stress. Other features of the situation will tell you which response is more likely.

Facial expressions also offer important clues. Is the dog avoiding eye contact or fixing you with a direct hard stare? Are the pupils dilated? Are the whites of the eyes showing ? (Sometimes described as whale eye.) Are the ears folded back, held at attention or relaxed? In many instances, dogs respond with their jaws, which reveal a great deal of emotion. Is the jaw tightly clenched or relaxed? Showing teeth is the classic sign of impending aggression, but it can also indicate submission depending on whether the lips are pulled upward to bare the teeth, or pulled back to produce a smile.

Body posture must also be evaluated within the context of other gestures regardless of whether the dog is standing, sitting, or lying down. Is the dog's overall demeanor calm, relaxed, tense, or stressed? Is the tail held, held high or low? Is it moving in a fast or slow wag, or tucked firmly between the legs? Is the dog's weight centered on the front or back feet? A calm dog will have all four feet planted firmly with equal weight distribution. A weight shift to the back legs indicates the dog is ready for action. Weight balanced on the front feet, standing on tiptoes, can indicate a shift to a dominant demeanor.

Whining is used to signify distress or deference to a social superior. Growling signifies a defensive or offensive warning. Barking is a neutral vocal signal and dogs use it for multiple functions ranging from an attention getting device to an outlet to relieve anxiety.

Rewards

Rewards can be defined as anything your dog actually values; praise, food, toys, or play, anything your Dachshund loves will qualify. The type of reward you use will depend on your Dachshund's personality and what you are trying to teach. Access to playmates or a car ride can become a training incentive. The most important rule is that the dog perceives the reward as more interesting and valuable compared to competing distractions in the environment.

Rewards may also be too weak or strong to make them useful in a training context even if they appeal to your dog. Some dogs become too excited or distracted by food. On the other hand, petting and praise can help get the dog on your page but are not always sufficient to maintain focus. They may also be counter-productive for a hyperactive dog that habitually becomes overexcited.

Food Rewards

Treats are the most reliable reward. Their message is immediate and unambiguous. They also serve a dual purpose as both a reward and an attention-getting device. Displaying the treat implies that the reward is imminent and most dogs quickly decide that a food reward is always possible, regardless of whether it is visible. Rewarding good behavior with a treat increases the likelihood that it will be repeated, but as we will see, the actual process is slightly more complicated.

Intermittent Reward Schedules

Every dog would be perfectly trained if it required nothing more than bribery.

Using rewards properly includes knowing when to give them less often and when to vary them with other, less powerful reinforcements. Frustration enhances a dog's motivation to a certain point. Shifting from a continuous to a variable reinforcement schedule is not a random decision when you are training a Dachshund.

Provide treats frequently when first teaching something new, possibly as often as one per second. Eventually, switch to a variable reinforcement rate to maintain the behavior or encourage a higher performance level. Of course, there are exceptions to this, such as when reinforcing a

For most Dachshunds, food is the best reward.

Training Tip

Soft, bite-sized food treats work best. They should be extremely tasty and small enough to be chewed and swallowed in a second. You will be using a lot of them. Being completely stuffed with treats will not enhance motivation. For example, a single turkey frank should yield at least 50 treats. Nutritional value should also be a consideration. Dachshunds are prone to obesity. Treats should never comprise more than ten percent of the dog's diet. Tiny pieces of high quality foods such as lean meat, chicken, or cheese are good choices.

behavior at a distance or instilling long duration for a response.

Sustaining Motivation

As your Dachshund's response becomes more reliable, intermittent rewards will maintain focus and improve performance because a degree of frustration spurs the dog to try a bit harder. You still need to give them occasionally, especially if the dog begins showing signs of boredom or distraction. According to classical conditioning a behavior that is not occasionally rewarded will diminish. According to operant conditioning, intermittently reinforcing a behavior produces a more stable response. Good training utilizes both.

Because dogs are naturally opportunistic, they always remain attuned to the possibility of a reward. This can work both ways. It is possible for dogs to become bored with a predictable reward or start looking for ways to improve the situation. Trainers sometimes try to solve this by upping the ante and providing increasingly tasty rewards. This may work for a while but there is an ultimate limit to the appeal of any reward. Dispensing and withholding them is far more effective because the dog's expectations remain uniformly high.

Clicker Training

Clicker training teaches your Dachshund to respond to something meaningless—a click—by associating it with something valuable—food. Through conditioning, the dog responds to the click with enthusiasm normally reserved for food. The

Five Steps to Success

1. *Set up situations where your dog is likely to succeed more often than not. Setting goals too high invites failure.*
2. *Reward every successful response until the behavior becomes totally reliable.*
3. *Once reliability has been established phase out the rewards for one quarter of the responses. As long as the behavior remains stable, cut back to rewarding half of the best responses.*
4. *Eventually, this can be further reduced to rewarding only a quarter or fifth of the responses.*
5. *This initial frustration should motivate the dog to an improved level of performance. However, that is not an infallible Dachshund rule. If at any time your dog begins regressing you will need to step back and raise your level of reinforcement again.*

advantage of this method is that the reinforcement can be offered almost simultaneously as the behavior occurs.

■ The first step is known as *charging*, teaching the dog to make a positive association about the clicker. Simply click and immediately reward your Dachshund for every attentive response. An easily swallowed food treat works best. Timing is key to establishing this connection, so you don't want the dog to spend ten minutes chewing between clicks.

■ Give the treat as quickly as possible whenever the dog orients to the click. Do not click repeatedly if you don't get instant results. Giving more than one click per behavior runs the risk of confusing the dog. After fifteen or twenty rewards most Dachshunds have a firm grasp of the concept. They are sound sensitive and highly food-oriented, a perfect combination for clicker training.

- Keep in mind that every behavior that happens between the click and the treat can be inadvertently reinforced. Pay attention to what you are rewarding and add some variables to each training session to prevent the dog from forming a response to something totally irrelevant.
- When the click/reward connection is firmly established in the dog's mind you can use this response to shape your Dachshund's behavior by rewarding actions almost as fast as they happen.

Clicker training utilizes principles of both classical and operant conditioning and there is a tremendous overlap between these learned associations. In the long run, the involuntary response elicited through classical conditioning will override behaviors learned through operant conditioning. This means that when your Dachshund is weighing the choices of coming when called or making a mad dash for the neighbors' cat, a well-timed click can turn the tide.

The clicker is a helpful tool for some aspects of Dachshund training, but it's not always useful in every situation. It is excellent for encouraging focus and shaping a specific behavior. However, some dogs become too excited by clicker training which can be counterproductive if you are trying to instill a calm response such as during crate training.

A well-timed click can reinforce the response you are hoping for, such as encouraging an enthusiastic recall.

A clicker is not the most flexible training tool. In some instances, a clicker can become an awkward distraction, and actually get in the way of the training process. Plan on using it for more complex training.

Rules and Boundaries

A predictable routine sets a benchmark for acceptable behavior to help your Dachshund integrate into your daily life. Everyone in the household must be prepared to reinforce identical ground rules and respond consistently to the dog's behavior. Alternately ignoring and reprimanding a dog for the same thing will foster frustration, confusion, and anxiety.

On the other hand, if you are consistently paying attention and encouraging behaviors you want from your Dachshund, you won't have a lot of need for discipline. You can consistently provide subtle corrections—such as a well- timed *ah-ah* at the precise moment to interrupt bad behavior before it goes too far.

Of course occasions will crop up when that is not sufficient and a loud *NO*, accompanied by a leash correction or time out is needed to get the point across. Positive reinforcement is best in most situations but it won't inhibit unwanted behavior, especially those triggered by natural instinct.

Positive training methods are sometimes described as the natural way to train dogs, implying that negative reinforcement does not figure in the canine learning process. Anyone who has observed a mother dog interacting with her puppies knows this is a myth. Positive and negative reinforcement play equally important roles. The critical difference is way they are used. Most trainers lack the skill to properly use corrections and ultimately create problems through misuse. A reprimand must be immediate and unemotional but significant enough to immediately get your message across to halt the unwanted behavior. That does not make it an effective shortcut for training. Your Dachshund will stop a behavior in response to a reprimand but it does not disappear from the dog's memory.

Just as a mother dog reprimands her pup, punishment must be directly attached to the unwanted behavior to be effective. Even a two-minute interval between action and consequence will render it meaningless to the dog. Corrections must also be tailored to the dog's temperament, rather than the owner's emotional state. A confident dog might fail to notice a correction that would prove devastating to a soft, sensitive dog.

For instance, excessive barking might be due to boredom or generalized anxiety. A mild reprimand may encourage more barking from a demanding dog seeking attention. On the other hand, a harsh reprimand could easily intensify it by further intimidating a fearful dog. It is more effective to concentrate on rewarding behavior that puts your Dachshund on the path to figuring out what you want. This helps the dog develop awareness about the cause and effect relationship between actions and consequences.

Dachshund Training Ground Rules

1. Don't apply generalizations to any training situation.

Generalizing about temperament, behavior or motivation is not advisable when training any dog. However, it's not likely to backfire quite so spectacularly for breeds less inclined to variable behavior. Dachshunds are free thinkers and problem solvers. They fixate on details and instinctively innovate. They make very specific connections between cause and effect events.

The first step in revising unwanted behavior is discovering the underlying motivation.

■ Notice the circumstances and evolving patterns linked to the behavior
■ Accurately interpret the body language accompanying the behavior

■ Resist labeling and don't hesitate to think outside the box to find a solution

2. Respond to behavior as it occurs.

Dachshunds are often described as quirky because they are so sensitive to their environment. A myriad of subtle internal and external factors constantly influence their behavior. They are also quick to form learned associations. Competing motivations are always a training issue but this is more pronounced in Dachshunds. Unlike breeds that prioritize social approval, a Dachshund tends to be primarily responsive to the environment. You won't even be aware of many of the factors motivating your dog at any given moment.

Both instinctive and learned behaviors are reinforced by rewards in the dog's environment. This happens continually. A good portion of training involves replacing the dog's natural response with something that is, for the dog, unnatural. This will not be possible unless you understand the motivation and the payoff. This is also why training fails when it is limited to classes or lessons. Your Dachshund has no reason to transfer skills learned in a formal class to daily life situations. Facilitating this transition is your responsibility. Get in the habit of managing your Dachshund's behavior with consistent reinforcement, feedback to interrupt unwanted behavior, and tools to prevent the dog from losing control.

3. Evaluate each situation from your Dachshund's perspective.

Dogs prioritize every situation according to their immediate perceptions, mood, and stress levels. Simply telling your Dachshund to ignore the squirrels and come in the house is unlikely to have much impact. The dog may be totally aroused and completely oblivious to you. Or, your increasingly impatient reaction may telegraph stress further escalating the dog's arousal. This has nothing to do with being stubborn or uncooperative although it may seem that way when you are chasing your demon wiener around the yard. An impulsive rather than a detached response to your dog's actions creates a good deal of frustration for both of you.

4. Think outside the box

Training is not something you do *to* your Dachshund; it is something you do *with* your Dachshund. Have a choice of training tools ready to address various situations. Dachshunds are programmed to think outside the box and you must get into the same habit. Training should transcend the idea of giving or responding to commands and become a working partnership. As you forge a better connection with your dog you will find yourself discarding many preconceived notions about the process and refining your methods to respond to your dog. Never hesitate to be creative.

If a certain approach fails to yield results, try something else. Also get into the habit of assessing what you may be doing wrong.

■ Was the dog too anxious or excited to focus?
■ Were you providing sufficient reinforcement?
■ Were you pushing the dog to the next level of training a little too soon?

4 Living the Dachshund Life

Introducing Your Dachshund to Her New Home

Regardless of whether your new Dachshund is a puppy or an adult, you must provide the tools to ensure a successful transition into your household. This means incorporating your dog into your routine. It may sound simple, but Dachshunds have a reliable tendency to get into everything if not carefully supervised. They are notorious for trying to eat indigestible items. Many are also adept escape artists. Supervision is the only way to prevent these and other potentially dangerous behaviors. You must simultaneously provide learning opportunities, put boundaries in place, and reinforce rules. It's a tricky situation, but necessary if your Dachshund is to formulate a successful survival strategy.

Socialization Strategies

In the wild, young animals are forced to assimilate huge amounts of information to formulate survival strategies. Equipped with the motivation to investigate their environment as soon as they can walk, they also posses a mental resiliency and learning capacity that will not be as sharp later in life. This is not a coincidence. Nature has equipped them for fast-track learning when it counts most. The mental framework that a puppy develops during the first three months of life defines perceptions, motivations, and response levels throughout the dog's entire life.

With adequate learning experience during these months, almost every dog can successfully acclimate to a variety of lifestyles. Previous learning can always be revised through subsequent behavior modification, but later training will never compensate for a lack of early learning experiences.

For young animals in the wild, learning opportunities arrive on a disconcertingly regular basis. This is not the case for domestic dogs. To improve your puppy's memory skills, cognitive function, confidence, and mental resilience during this formative period, you must systematically provide environmental challenges. A puppy's conflicting reactions when investigating something new illustrates the amount of learning taking place. The unfamiliar person or object will be initially avoided, then approached cautiously, thoroughly investigated, and eventually ignored. These exploratory tactics change as the dog matures, but always follow a pattern of testing, checking, analyzing, refining the approach, and making a final determination—exactly the same response pattern that adult animals use to calculate safety.

Socialization Strategies For Puppies 8–16 Weeks

Start socializing your pup as earlier as possible. Avoid places where dogs congregate until your pup's vaccinations are complete, but don't wait until then to begin the socialization process. Those wasted weeks cannot be replaced.

- Familiarize your puppy with a wide range of indoor and outdoor environments including parks, beaches, busy sidewalks, and other public areas.
- Have your puppy meet a variety of people of different ages, nationalities, and gender (dogs definitely recognize the difference between men and women).
- Supply opportunities to safely interact with other species—especially different breeds of dogs
- Provide mental and physical challenges. These don't need to be complicated and should be geared to challenge, but not overwhelm, your pup's mental and emotional thresholds. For instance, figuring out how to escape from a cardboard box is a great learning experience for a puppy.
- If you plan to have your dog compete in organized dog sports provide positive introductions to all aspects of this lifestyle.

Generalized Socialization

To a certain degree, familiarity with a variety of people, places, and things produces comprehensive socialization. However, generalized association has never been the greatest attribute of the canine mind. Failing to recognize a well-known

> ### Socialization Timeline
> - *At three weeks puppies become responsive to social interaction and begin exploring their environment.*
> - *By eight weeks they are intensely curious and highly responsive to new experiences.*
> - *Between 12 and 16 weeks this acceptance phase wanes and natural wariness emerges.*

Stealing food is a minor crime compared to some of the trouble an unsupervised Dachshund can get into.

person who suddenly appears wearing a strange hat is a typical example. Therefore you must have tools ready to manage these situations when necessary. An apprehensive puppy instinctively turns to the pack leader for direction and reassurance. Your targeting and relaxation tools must provide this.

Meeting People

Because many Dachshunds are naturally aloof, wariness towards unfamiliar people is common. To prevent this, puppies should be consistently socialized. Some Dachshunds require more encouragement than others, and the process must be more intensive for them to become adequately socialized to people. This is based on individual temperament, environment, and genetics. In addition to early life experiences, these variations are traceable to individual neurological and hormonal patterns. Some puppies become well socialized through as little as 20 minutes of interaction with people twice a week. This will be profoundly inadequate for pups that are inherently timid or aloof.

Puppies deprived of human contact during their first three months will remain permanently fearful of people regardless of later training and socialization. They will always resort to an instinctive fight or flight response when confronted or stressed.

■ As long as puppies have had some introduction to humans by seven weeks of age they can be socialized to accept humans after ten weeks of age. However, socialization at a later age never totally compensates for earlier deprivation.

Training Tip

Eliciting prey drive by initiating play is a good way to shift a dog from an anxious to happy state of mind. Controlling toys and play times makes this easier. It may not be possible if your Dachshund constantly has access to every toy. By restricting access, your puppy will be attuned to the idea of shifting instantly into play mode when seeing a particular toy or hearing a key word like "playtime." Very often, the mere sight of a beloved plaything is enough to interrupt an impending anxiety attack. When you see your Dachshund beginning to tense up, pull out his favorite toy for a short game. Tug of war is a good choice because it not only shifts the dog's mood from defense to prey, it also alleviates tension and puts the dog's focus back on you. From your Dachshund's point of view, the two of you have become a pack working together to kill prey and this instinctive drive trumps just about any other environmental stimuli.

■ Ideally, puppies should receive consistent, comprehensive socialization from the commencement of their early learning phase until adulthood. Otherwise, even well socialized puppies may regress during later stages of fear and shyness.

Wariness

Wariness and shyness are often confused. Several genetic traits are responsible for a dog's instinctive desire to approach and interact. Although they act in concert,

Training Tip

A common Dachshund problem is the habit of dashing out the door as soon as it's opened a crack. This is not only annoying, but dangerous. Your Dachshund should only step outdoors when you give permission.

- *Put a leash on the dog, position yourself in the doorway, and open the door slightly.*
- *When the dog tries to dash through, close it.*
- *After a few attempts the dog will hesitate before barreling on through.*
- *As soon as you see this hesitation, praise and reward the response.*
- *Continue interrupting the sequence with a well timed ah ah! and a closing door before the dog can get through the doorway.*
- *Reward the dog for stopping a foot or two from the doorway and waiting for your cue to step outside.*

whether a puppy has been neutered. Puppies are apt to become more territorial and less accepting of changes in their routine or environment at these times. This is usually temporary, and can be minimized by reinforcing socialization and habituation. Even well socialized puppies often require some degree of reinforcement during these months.

Unwarranted fear reactions usually diminish as puppies gain confidence through experience but can remain more pronounced in highly sensitive individuals. Many Dachshunds fall into this group. Some puppies require consistent exposure to unfamiliar people, places, sights, and sounds to prevent natural caution from evolving into timidity. Socialization strategies must be tailored to each pup's emotional threshold.

Reassurance of a Pack Leader

Dogs instinctively try to assimilate into a social pack. They have innate skills to do this, but cannot read minds, so you'll need to help your pup along. Be predictive, rather than reactive, as your Dachshund learns to assimilate into your family pack. Most importantly, be aware of learned associations that may form in response to the environment. Remember—operant conditioning can happen fast. A structured approach to manage the socialization and habituation process is the only way to keep on top of this. This requires effort and discipline and is definitely less fun than spontaneously responding. Puppies instinctively

these traits (boldness, curiosity, opportunism) are transmitted separately. Wariness of the unfamiliar is a basic survival strategy. Evolution has made it less pronounced in dogs, but like all animals, they are genetically programmed to become cautious as they mature.

The extent of this trait varies in Dachshunds. A puppy's socialization period starts waning at approximately three months, to be replaced by what is sometimes referred to as a fear-imprinting period. A second phase of wariness may emerge during adolescence, triggered by hormonal fluctuations regardless of

A Dachshund's behavior is constantly influenced by his environment.

instance, your Dachshund should eat and sleep where and when you designate, not the other way round. You, not the dog, are in charge of giving out toys and taking them away, initiating and ending play.

Simple steps like these will go a long way to prevent problems. Don't encourage attention-seeking behavior or demands like barking, jumping, pawing, or nipping. That does not mean you should ignore your Dachshund. (As if that could happen!) Just remember that your attention is a valuable reward; don't give it away for free or inadvertently use it to encourage bad habits. Use it to shape the behaviors you want.

A stable routine is important, but build some variations into it to encourage adaptability. Your goal is to create the security of predictable routine while encouraging acceptance of occasional changes. This should include leaving the dog alone for varied times. Shut the door and go to another room for a short time or go out to do a few errands.

Habituation for Adults

Every adult dog has habits. You may not be aware of them, but rest assured they exist and will complicate the adjustment process for adult Dachshunds. If your Dachshund arrives with a parcel of habits you want to change, expect three or four weeks of daily work to accomplish this. Habits are constructed from framework of varying experiences and competing motivations, and are therefore always susceptible to internal and external influences. They can be changed if you are prepared to make the effort. A house leash is a great tool to supervise a

look to their pack leader for direction in unfamiliar situations. Manage the environment to get the right message across.

The pack leader's status is acknowledged because he or she is in charge of the good stuff.

- Food
- Toys
- Play
- Territory
- Attention

Following a regular schedule rather than responding to the dog's demands will help establish you as the pack leader. For new dog habituating to a new environment. The dog should be confined or crated when you cannot supervise and should be at your side for as much time as possible.

Dachshunds and Children

Dachshunds are regularly recommended as companions for kids. However, good relationships between dogs and children don't happen automatically. A dog may misunderstand a child's unpredictable or abrupt mannerisms. A child has no way of understanding canine body language unless they have been taught what to look for. A children's dog training class is an excellent way to help a child learn techniques to successfully and safely interact with dogs.

It's equally important to implement ground rules and supervise. Children under age eight should always be supervised when playing with a dog. Older children should be encouraged to help with routine care such as feeding, walking, grooming, and training but should never be left solely in charge of dog care.

Safety Rules For Children and Dogs

- Never leave the dog on furniture or beds. If forgotten, the dog may be injured jumping or falling off.
- Avoid chasing or grabbing the dog even if it is meant in the spirit of fun. A startled dog can be frightened by a well-intentioned but unexpected hug.

Dachshunds and children can be a great combination but these relationships require ground rules and supervision.

- The dog is off limits when eating, sleeping, or crated.
- Children's friends are not permitted to play with the dog unless supervised by an adult.
- A child should never reprimand or punish the dog for misbehavior. Instruct the child to notify an adult rather than to attempt this.

Dachshunds and Other Pets

During their socialization period, puppies experience mixed imprinting, allowing them to form social relationships with other

Home Schooling

Housetraining

Puppies instinctively keep their sleeping area clean, and this behavior that can be reinforced through training. By four weeks of age pups will eliminate away from areas where they eat or sleep if given the opportunity. These early experiences will have a lifelong impact on a dog's elimination habits. After four months of age, established elimination patterns become more difficult to revise.

Reinforcing this natural instinct through careful supervision and positive reinforcement is far easier than revising bad habits later on. Although puppies leave their sleeping area to eliminate, once they are outside of this area elimination also takes on connotations of territorial marking. Inhibiting this instinct to eliminate throughout familiar territory is the goal of housetraining.

Dogs don't reliably generalize housetraining habits. These habits remain linked to immediate social and territorial circumstances. Regardless of whether you are introducing an adult or a puppy into your home, implement the same procedure.

- Restrict access to an area of your home where you can supervise.
- Crate or confine the dog when you cannot supervise.
- Take the dog to the elimination area at scheduled times. If she regularly has accidents at certain times, revise this schedule.
- Learn to spot telltale signs that the dog needs to go such as sniffing and circling. Intentional sniffing sucks odor particles directly into the dog's olfactory receptors, which triggers a neurological message in the bladder.
- Remain with dog. This is the only way to guarantee results. You can also reinforce elimination habits by immediately offering a treat afterwards. Using a key word or clicker also helps reinforce the message. Feedback must be immediate.
- Allow 15 to 20 minutes and minimize distractions until the dog goes. Dachshunds are easily distracted. For instance, if you customarily walk your Dachshund try to make sure elimination takes place at start of walk. Many dogs become distracted during a walk, don't relieve themselves and arrive home still needing to go.
- If you have no success in 20 minutes don't assume the dog did not need to go. Often, the dog will have an accident within minutes of getting back into the house. Put dog in crate for 30 minutes and repeat the process.
- Don't experiment with training methods if you don't get fast results. This can confuse the dog and prolong the process. Some puppies learn housetraining quickly; others can take quite a bit longer.
- Keep your expectations realistic especially if you are training a puppy. You are instilling mental habits first and the physical ability to conform to these habits will follow in time.
- A few successful experiences do not guarantee reliable housetraining. Continue supervising and reinforcing until the dog is a year old.

Some puppies can be housetrained in a few days, while others may need several months of supervision and reinforcement.

■ Carefully clean up all traces of odor after an accident. If you have other dogs, they may also begin doing the same. Even if you can't smell it, Dachshunds have an excellent scenting ability.

■ Reprimanding or punishing a dog for housetraining accidents is counterproductive and more likely to impart a completely different message, such as teaching the dog never to eliminate in your presence. At that point, housetraining becomes far more of a challenge.

Establish a Schedule

An eight-week-old puppy will need to eliminate every hour or two. Accidents will happen, but get the puppy to the proper location as often as possible. This schedule can gradually be reduced as the puppy matures. By five months of age, most puppies reliably relieve themselves at scheduled times but may require more training to prevent accidents indoors when they are distracted or excited. Puppies should also be able to sleep through the night in the crate without a bathroom break by this age. Adults should be exercised morning, midday, early evening, and before bed.

If your pup regularly needs to go out in the middle of the night, don't provide the chance for accidents in the crate. Take the pup out but don't let this become a habit unless you are a night owl. Try feeding earlier, restricting water intake for an hour or two before bedtime and ensuring that the pup is tired out by bedtime.

If forgotten on a sofa or bed, a puppy can be injured if trying to jump off on his or her own.

species. Their biological imperative to socialize easily extends to other species until the dog is about four months old. Through intensive socialization during these weeks, instinctive predator/prey relationships can be revised into social attachments.

After the close of this socialization period, it may not be possible to reliably socialize Dachshunds to other species. This can be a major concern for Dachshunds with high predatory drive that will be expected to cohabit with other pets such as cats, birds, or rodents.

The fact that a Dachshund willingly accepts familiar animals as part of their pack doesn't guarantee tolerance towards other species outside of the pack. A Dachshund may always regard unfamiliar animals as fair game regardless of training and socialization. Predatory behavior is the most difficult type of aggression to modify because it is self-reinforcing.

Crate Training

Crate training reinforces the canine instinct to seek a safe den. Rather than perceiving it as incarceration, dogs enjoy small, confined spots for privacy and security. Done properly, this instinct is easily translated into crate training.

A crate offers several training advantages:

■ It is a safe comfortable place to leave the dog when you cannot supervise.

Training Tip

Create a positive association with the crate by encouraging your Dachshund to eat in the crate. Reserve a special, enticing chew toy that is only offered to the dog when crated.

- *Encourage the dog to investigate the crate with the door open.*
- *When the dog seems interested, toss a treat in the crate and give a command such as "Enter" or "Crate" to encourage the dog to enter.*
- *When the dog complies, immediately give a command to come out of the crate.*
- *Immediately toss in another treat. After ten repeats your Dachshund should willingly enter crate anticipating a treat while becoming equally reluctant to come out because there is no treat waiting on that end.*
- *You can reinforce this by giving a "Relax" command if the dog chooses to remain in the crate.*
- *After doing this exercise for two days, add the step of closing the door and leave the dog for 30 minutes. If your Dachshund responds with barking or whining, ignore this behavior and it will subside. Never respond by immediately letting the dog out.*
- *When the dog has been quiet for 30 minutes open the door and give a command to come out. Be careful not to encourage excited behavior when the dog comes out. Keep it low key.*
- *Gradually add daily time until the dog can stay crated for three or four hours.*

- It prevents the dog from doing damage or getting injured in your absence.
- It prevents accidental escapes when you have workmen in your home likely to leave doors and gates ajar.
- It is essential for safely transporting your dog by car.
- It simplifies housetraining because the dog is naturally reluctant to eliminate in crate.
- It provides a place for time out if the dog needs to calm down or deal with a fearful situation
- It allows the dog to be confined without feeling isolated.

Choose a plastic or wire crate large enough for the dog to stand erect and turn around. An overly large crate is not safe for travel and will be useless for

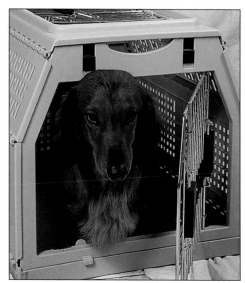

Leave the door open when first introducing your Dachshund to the crate.

Use a special command when training your dog to come out of the crate.

housetraining. It should be situated where the dog can view your household routine. Many owners move the crate to the bedroom at night for extra supervision. It should be furnished with a mat or blanket and a couple of chew toys. Choose them carefully. Some Dachshunds will chew and ingest bedding or toys. This can lead to potentially fatal choking or gastrointestinal blockage. Observe carefully when you give your Dachshund a new bed or toy and remove it if necessary.

Cooperating for Grooming

Every dog will need to be carried or restrained at some point for grooming or veterinary care. Dachshunds are built to wiggle out of tight spaces and they can be extremely difficult to hold when they choose not to cooperate. A panicky struggling dog can bite or be injured if dropped.

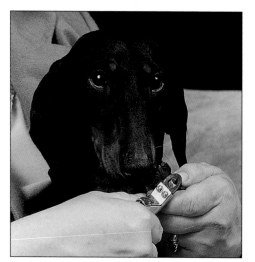

Don't expect your Dachshund to calmly tolerate nail clipping unless you have trained him to accept the procedure.

Dental care is a crucial aspect of health maintenance. Very few dogs accept this unless they have been trained to do so.

Training your Dachshund to accept being held is especially important if you have children. A child may impulsively hug or grab the dog and can be bitten if the dog panics. A Dachshund that is trained to accept being touched makes it easier for regularly evaluating health and condition, and noticing when something is wrong. If a normally cooperative dog suddenly avoids being touched it's a good indication of severe pain. If your Dachshund is intolerant of handling or restraint, do not assume that it is a temporary problem that will resolve itself. It will worsen unless you step in.

Avoiding Bad Eating Habits

Food can be a great reinforcement tool, but it can also trigger behavior problems from aggression to anorexia. Through operant conditioning a puppy learns the social and psychological connotations of food. Your Dachshund can use this to manipulate you unless you understand the rules of canine dining.

■ Dogs are natural scavengers, instinctively programmed to eat a variety of foods as part of their survival strategy.

■ Dogs are biologically and socially conditioned to bolt their food. From birth they learn to eat competitively. Puppies eat until they are exhausted, not until they are full. These habits do not diminish with maturity.

■ Their digestive systems accommodate this behavior. Carnivore teeth are designed for tearing rather than chewing. The canine esophagus is lined with

47

muscle fibers to push large amounts of poorly chewed food to the stomach. Dogs are also equipped with large stomachs and very short intestinal tracts to quickly digest big meals.

■ Dogs also possess the ability to vomit at will. This operates as a protective mechanism to prevent ingestion of toxic substances. It also allows them to vomit when they overeat, become overexcited, stressed, or frightened.

A structured feeding routine puts a psychological mechanism in place to discourage these innate habits. Remember: classical conditioning will override operant conditioning. Dogs are creatures of habit, and easily become accustomed to eating a particular food, in measured amounts, at specified times. This not only reinforces good eating habits and housetraining routines. Conditioned response also plays a major role in stimulating a healthy appetite.

Puppies are instinctively conditioned to compete with their littermates during mealtime.

Feed your Dachshund at the same time in a location relatively free of distractions to encourage calmness and security.

Free feeding is diametrically opposed to a dog's mentally or physically conditioned eating habits. Depending on age, your Dachshund should be offered one to three measured portions of food per day. These should be consumed within ten or fifteen minutes. Many dogs bolt it down in a couple of minutes.

As a general rule, Dachshunds are not fussy eaters, so any lack of appetite on your pet's part may simply be due to overfeeding. Most owners are far more likely to overfeed than underfeed, making obesity the number one dietary problem affecting pet dogs in this country. Your vet or breeder can advise you concerning your Dachshund's ideal weight and portion size. A waistline should be visible, you should be able to feel ribs beneath the coat, and the dog should not waddle when walking. The feeding amounts listed on dog food packages are merely recommendations, and tend to err on the side of generosity.

Physical reasons for a reduced appetite range from stress, hot weather, teething or periodontal disease, recent vaccinations, or more serious health issues. If the problem persists for more than a couple of days a vet exam is in order. Poor appetite can be the earliest indication of illness.

Car Travel with Your Dachshund

Dogs typically love riding in the car from the first experience. For those who find the ride enjoyable, a car trip can become a very effective reward. For dogs not socialized to find this a fun experience, the mere thought of entering a car can trigger panic. At some point every dog will face a car trip for one reason or another and positive introduction should be part of your puppy's socialization routine. It's a great way to socialize pups that have not completed their vaccinations and a good adjunct to crate training.

Acclimating Your Dachshund to Car Travel

■ Your Dachshund should ride in a crate, with absorbent bedding in case of motion sickness and a chew toy for distraction. A loose dog in the car is an invitation to disaster. A deployed airbag can kill a Dachshund instantly.

■ Make sure the crate is stabilized to prevent it from falling or bouncing while you drive. Avoid driving moves likely to trigger fear or nausea.

■ Start with short trips. Take the dog along when you do local errands.

■ Reassure the dog during the ride and include some fun destinations like a trip to the park.

■ If the dog becomes panicky or ill, cut the trip short and try again the next day. Don't give up. Dogs will not overcome this problem without ongoing conditioning.

Motion Sickness

Motion sickness occurs when detectors in the balance and ocular centers of brain

Dachshunds can be quite adventurous, as long as they have been trained to accept new and unusual experiences.

emit conflicting signals, leading to drooling, retching, vomiting, and occasionally diarrhea. Many dogs experience this problem as puppies but outgrow it. To help prevent the problem follow these guidelines:

■ Do not feed the dog before the trip.

■ Keep the car cool and well ventilated.

■ Try a wire crate, car seat or doggy seat belt, all of which allow the dog to see out of windows while secured.

■ Try natural nausea remedies such as ginger cookies or soothe anxiety with herbal or floral extracts such as Rescue Remedy (found in health food stores).

■ Consult your vet about administering motion sickness medications such as Benadryl, Bonine, or Dramamine.

49

5 *Dachshund To Dachshund*

Throughout evolution, humans and dogs have shared both a preference for group living and the development of behaviors that facilitate such an arrangement. Teamwork is instinctive to both dogs and humans due to its survival advantage. For the modern domestic dog, pack membership is no longer necessary to ensure survival, but dogs, like humans, still retain a need for social acceptance. Recognize it, accept it, and make it work to your mutual advantage.

Socializing Your Dachshund to Other Dogs

Puppies are mentally equipped to bond with other species during their socialization period, but circumstances dictate the bonds that ultimately develop. A dog's social identity forms through a multi-faceted process. Ideally puppies should experience both human and canine interaction during these formative weeks. If deprived of adequate human contact, dogs will develop a preference for dogs. and their subsequent interest in humans will diminish. This does not automatically lead to fear or shyness. These dogs will tolerate people, but lack the

capacity to form genuine attachments. This makes them less responsive to training because they lack motivation to communicate with humans or seek approval. Lack of canine social interaction can have an equally negative impact.

A puppy's bond to its mother is triggered by the positive association of body contact, warmth, and food. This not only increases the puppy's survival odds, it creates a preference. Puppies are not born with an innate sense of identity. They have an instinctive need for social contact, but possess no natural awareness of the fact that they are dogs. This association is learned and can be misdirected.

Under normal circumstances, puppies learn the basics of social interaction from their dam, littermates, and other dogs during their early weeks. This contact is essential until they are at least six weeks old.

It is possible for a dog to function without basic canine social skills, but it will become a constant source of stress. An imperfect understanding of canine communication gestures will lead to ongoing communication problems.

Dogs have adopted shortcuts, known as ritualized behavior, to communicate and manipulate social interactions. Through ritualization, typical canine gestures are

Dominant and submissive dogs exhibit distinctive body language.

stylized to communicate unmistakable messages.

All types of significant social information are conveyed this way, such as courtship, play, and threats. It contributes to pack welfare by minimizing aggression and conflict. For instance, aggressive confrontation is transformed into a dramatic display of bared teeth, raised hackles, staring, posturing, and growling, all of which rarely escalate into actual conflict. Often, these intense gestures are enough to settle the matter. When it does escalate into an actual fight, three-quarters of the outcome is decided beforehand through blustering and posturing. Both dogs reach an understanding about the likely outcome, either by acknowledging superior rank, or mutual agreement of who would probably win.

The first ritualized gesture puppies learn is one of the most important: appeasement. This tactic is used to deflect aggression by displaying submission to higher-ranking pack members. Puppies learn this from their dam during weaning, but soon start using it in many situations to avoid aggression, including interactions with humans. If they don't have the oppor-

tunity to learn it, they must rely on the old instinctive standby of fight or flight when threatened. Nor will they be able to recognize when another dog is trying to deflect aggression in this way.

Without early social experiences, puppies remain handicapped in their ability to relate to both humans and other dogs. They also need ongoing practice to perfect these skills; otherwise their interactions will remain awkward and inappropriate. Puppies are routinely corrected by older dogs for behavior like rough play, hard biting, or excessively familiar greetings.

Ensuring Ample Canine Contact

If your Dachshund is your only dog, interaction with other dogs should be a regular feature of the socialization process. Not only does it improve communication skills, it also prevents fear of other dogs. Poorly socialized dogs are not necessarily fearful around other dogs, but may behave inappropriately due to anxiety.

Dog Parks

Dog parks offer endless opportunities for your Dachshund to socialize with other dogs. In many urban areas these fenced public spaces represent the only opportunity for dogs to engage in off-lead play. They provide a reasonably risk-free environment, but that doesn't mean supervision isn't necessary. The friendly, relaxed atmosphere also encourages owners to mingle rather than to pay attention to what their dogs are up to. Nor are the parks ideally suited to every dog.

Evaluating the Dog Park

Before you let your dog run free in a dog park, take a good look at the surroundings. Entrances should have double gates and fencing should prevent dogs from jumping over or squeezing underneath. Segregated play areas for large and small dogs should be clearly designated and fenced.

Good sanitation is essential. Disease can spread like wildfire in these high-density environments. Owners should clean up after their dogs and hard surfaces should be disinfected frequently. Clean-up tools, disinfectant, plastic bags, and receptacles should be available.

Some dog parks are open to the general public; others require membership. Most require proof of vaccination or restrict the number of dogs one person can bring.

Dogs are usually required to wear a visible form of identification. To prevent fights most parks also ban bitches in season, overly rough or aggressive dogs, and personal dog toys and treats. Nothing will ensure safety more than conscientious owners paying close attention to their dogs.

- Conscientious owners clean up after their dogs.
- Conscientious owners leave dogs that may be carrying contagious illness at home.
- Conscientious owners immediately intervene to stop rough play or aggression.
- Conscientious owners don't allow their dogs to harass anyone—human or canine.

Rules for Play

Dog play is a gruesome spectacle of lunging, pouncing, and throat grabbing accompanied by horrific shrieks, growls, and barks. It can be hard to tell when things really are getting out of hand because most of it looks incredibly savage from a human perspective. Dogs can become totally unresponsive in this aroused state and what began as play can quickly transform into aggression. To keep things from escalating keep the following in mind.

- Restrict play to dogs similar in size, energy level, and temperament. Wrestling and pouncing can be dangerous for dogs that are not well matched in weight, size, and strength.
- If the play seems one-sided put a stop to it. One dog should not be singled out for repeated chasing. If one dog persistently seeks a hiding place, it is not having fun.
- A painful yelp should halt the action. If it doesn't, don't hesitate to step into the situation and call a time-out for safety.

Poor communication, inappropriate responses, and misplaced anxiety are major contributors to dog park altercations. Immature puppies and poorly socialized

These pups appear to be fighting, but other aspects of their body language reveal their playful intentions.

dogs are more likely to overstep the boundaries of acceptable play in a group situation. This can trigger unwarranted fight or flight reactions. For instance, puppies of both sexes often mount each other during play. An adult dog may interpret this as an attempt at dominance and trigger fighting.

Canine body language can also be misinterpreted between breeds, leading to unpredictable results. Gestures vary due to anatomical or behavioral diversity causing problems between even well socialized dogs. For instance, a Dachshund can misinterpret the upright posture of normal Boxer demeanor as a challenge and respond aggressively towards a dog that was simply minding its own business. Tail signals, such as a wag that is loose, relaxed, and friendly or one that is high, fast, and

menacing, can be a good indicator of mood, but these gestures are not readily apparent on breeds with docked or short tails. Long, pendulous ears don't easily convey a dominant message but the pert ears of a Chihuahua broadcast that message all the time. Likewise, raised hackles mean little with hairless breeds.

Some Dachshunds simply don't enjoy running around and roughhousing with unfamiliar dogs. If your dog really doesn't enjoy visiting the dog park don't do it.

Aggression Toward Strange Dogs

A few Dachshunds are so uncomfortable around strange dogs they resort to aggression. Defensive reactions such as growling, snapping, or lunging usually become a problem during adolescence, but often the initial motivation and numerous warning

The dog park can be a great place for your Dachshund to socialize with other breeds, but constant supervision is essential.

signs were present much earlier. Keeping dog on dog aggression in check requires vigilance on your part.

- Avoid situations that trigger aggression such as being fenced or leashed, or being placed in proximity to rough play at dog parks.
- Intervene at the earliest indication of aggression; don't allow things to escalate out of control.
- When correcting your dog in these situations be quick, calm, and firm. Never threaten the dog or behave excitedly as you intervene; doing so may reinforce aggression, boosting your dog's confidence or escalating the initial excitement.
- Teach your dog to focus and shift from an aggressive state by giving the *look* or *settle* command. Long-term behavior modification may be necessary to foster a calm, trusting response around other dogs. (See Chapter 9.)

Dog Fights

Dachshunds are inherently courageous and not inclined to back down from a fight. This can be especially dangerous if the opponent is substantially larger.

If your Dachshund normally engages in group play, don't wait for an emergency; have a plan in place to stop a fight. A dog in the grip of defensive aggression is unlikely to be responsive, and even a small dog can inflict a serious bite. If you have no choice but physical intervention, grab a hind leg or tail, and put distance between the dogs A.S.A.P. Do not put yourself between the dogs unless you have the confidence to manage the situation. It is safer to spray the dogs with a hose or startle them with loud noise. Citronella spray or throwing a coat or blanket over one of the dogs may distract them for a moment.

Meet-ups can be the perfect alternative for Dachshund socialization.

Once they are separated, restrain them, turn them away from each other, and remove them immediately. If you stay put the dogs may reengage, redirect their aggression to another target, or other dogs on the scene may decide to join in.

Meet-Ups

Meet-ups are social events organized in a public place for a particular breed. This alleviates some of the problems of mixing dogs of varying size and temperament. These groups originated as owners of various breeds met regularly and formed friendships at public dog parks. The Internet allowed this to expand into structured groups all over the country that meet once or twice per month.

There are presently 82 Dachshund Meet-Up groups in 78 cities, providing great social and educational outlets for both humans and dogs. Join one and you'll not only have enjoyment of watching the dogs play, you'll also get the chance to swap Dachshund stories and discuss breed-related issues. Novice owners can find a network of support and information on local dog-care services. Larger groups organize more formal events, such as presentations by expert speakers on health and training topics. Many also raise funds for local Dachshund rescue groups through costume contests, Dachshund races, or Oktoberfest celebrations.

Doggy Daycare

Daycare is fast becoming the premier pet care option for working owners. It's a great way to socialize a timid dog to people and other dogs while preventing your Dachshund from being lonely or bored during the day. Most large cities have a range of daycare facilities. Some are run by veterinarians, boarding kennels, or grooming salons; others are independent ventures without previous experience managing large groups of dogs. Since the quality of care and facilities varies, it's essential to carefully check the provider's credentials.

Ask for recommendations and visit the facility to check it out. The premises should look and smell clean, with secure fencing and double gates at all entrances. Dogs should be exercised and kept in compatible manageable groups that can be carefully supervised. Some daycare programs offer enrichment activities for the dogs, which require a greater degree of supervision.

Staff members should be trained in health basics as well as emergency procedures. They should have a good understanding of canine behavior and be able to spot potential behavior problems. Pay attention to the techniques they use managing the difficult dogs, not just the sweet, placid ones their care groups. Most daycare facilities don't accept dogs with known behavior problems but there is always a risk when unfamiliar dogs mix.

Care providers should provide individual time for each dog as needed, and intervene effectively if the overall energy level of the group gets too high to ensure safety. The dogs should never be running the show. They should understand that there are rules and boundaries rather than perceiving the situation as an all day free for all. An unstructured, frenzied environment can easily undo all the work and training you have done with your Dachshund.

Play Dates

A familiar dog that can be available for play dates is the ideal solution for your Dachshund's canine socialization. Of course, this requires time and effort to find a suitable playmate and arrange visits. Many Dachshund owners consider adding a second dog to their household instead.

Multi-Dachshund Homes

Tips On Adding A New Dog To Your Household

- Conflict is less likely if you introduce a new dog of a different age and sex.
- If you choose another breed, the size, temperament, and energy levels should be comparable to a Dachshund.
- Give the dogs adequate time to bond. This may take up to three weeks. Do not push them into friendship by insisting that they eat or sleep together or share toys.
- Allow the dogs to become friends at their own pace and don't show favoritism towards a new dog through a greater share of attention.
- Even if they seem to be fine together, keep them separated when you cannot supervise.
- Toys, food, or other items that may incite possessiveness should only be available when you can supervise.

The Pack

Superficially, wolf and dog packs are similar but the differences define everything

Most puppies establish a social rank through regular interaction.

that sets the species apart. Wolf hierarchy is rigid and predictable. Rank is dictated by age, sex, and strength. The pack is structured around cooperative survival strategies to procure food, defend territory, and raise young. These factors don't figure in to the lives of most domestic dogs and this sort of thinking has pretty much gone out of style for them. They are far less concerned with long-range survival and far more interested in the immediate social implications of rank. Never underestimate the amount of time dogs devote to this.

- Puppies begin experimenting social gestures by six weeks of age.
- The earliest demonstrations of pack mentality invariably relate to food guarding, which can start at five weeks.
- By two months of age, play fighting can take on overtones of real pack behavior, with two or more puppies attacking weaker littermates.

Dominance and Rivalries

Canine social structures are unique, governed by circumstance. Domestic dog packs not only include more than one species but are constantly revised in response to internal and external influences.

Although the mechanics of a dog pack cannot be compared to the social hierarchy of wolves, it is a mistake to assume that pack mentality is superfluous to understanding canine motives. Like wolves, dogs have no desire for autonomy. Their contentment is contingent on a state of emotional dependence. Most dogs happily occupy a subordinate role because of the reassurance it provides. Their primary concerns are acceptance and social contact. Dogs employ subtle and sophisticated strategies to maintain these in the face of varying influences and it can get complicated. A domestic pack can include more

57

than one dominant individual, not necessarily a male. It is also possible for several dogs to behave as if they possessed dominant status. Sometimes this role is interchangeable; transferred to different individuals depending on what they are up to. One dog may be in charge when defending the territorial perimeter of the backyard. Another may assume leadership during mealtime. Rank can be contingent on which room of the house they are in, or which article of furniture they happen to be lying on.

It is also normal for several individuals to vie for identical status within the pack, resulting in almost continuous low-level conflict over food, territory, or attention. Most dogfights are actually the culmination of many phases of conflict to define status when an owner fails to implement and maintain pack order.

■ Owners are often unaware of the complicated social network operating under the radar. Most of the time peace reigns, in spite of subtle conflicts and competitions within the pack. Many factors can push the status quo past the breaking point. Minor incidents over food, toys, or territory can gradually escalate into fighting because they are overlooked or ignored by the pack leader. Hostility may ramp up quickly when a new dog is introduced, thereby upsetting pack order. Mature dogs are not uniformly tolerant of rambunctious puppies and this also triggers a fair number of conflicts.

■ Owners may unwittingly exacerbate the tension by creating situations that encourage aggression such as forcing the dogs to eat together or share toys.

■ Most conflicts involve two specific dogs regardless of how many live in the household.

■ These two dogs are usually the same sex. Fights between males are more common but fights between females tend to be more severe, triggered and motivated by bigger issues.

■ The dogs are usually between one and three years of age. Conflict can start when a puppy becomes more assertive with maturity, or when a formerly dominant dog begins to lose authority due to age or illness. An occasional fight within your pack can be attributed to your poor management skills as pack leader. If it becomes a habit, you need to take serious stock of what is going on behind the scenes.

Assess the factors contributing to the fighting.

■ Did the problem begin when a new dog or person entered the household?

■ Has the regular canine territory of your household recently changed?

■ Does one dog usually provoke the fights?

■ Do the altercations occur at a specific point in the daily routine or a specific room of the house?

■ How often do aggressive encounters take place? This may happen more often than you realize if you fail to notice subtle aggressive interactions.

■ How do the dogs behave towards each other at other times?

■ How do you typically react to the situation?

If you are an effective pack leader your dogs should immediately halt any behavior when you step in. This is probably the biggest test of your authority and if you don't measure up do not look for instant remedies. Dachshunds are highly sensitive to correction. Stepping in to stop a fight is fine but it must be done calmly and efficiently. Timing and intensity must be accurately calculated to effectively impart the appropriate message with unmistakable authority. Otherwise, you will contribute to the frenzied, aggressive atmosphere and unintentionally make matters worse. Frightening the dogs can easily reinforce reactions of defensive aggression or encourage the dominant dog to continue.

Discouraging Aggression

- When introducing a new dog into a multi-dog household you must vigilantly supervise the process and be capable of maintaining physical control of the dogs. This is your job as pack leader.
- Manage the environment to prevent aggression. The more often aggressive episodes occur, the more likely they will recur. This doesn't necessarily need to fit the classic signs of bullying. A fearful dog may successfully frighten another dog to keep it at a distance. Regardless of the motivation, if the strategy works, the dog will resort to it again.
- As pack leader, it is your responsibility to resolve conflicts and manage resources. A zero-tolerance approach must be your consistent policy in response to dog squabbles. Remove all items likely to trigger fights such as toys, bones, trashcans, and your personal possessions.

- Supervised social interactions help to enforce stability in the canine hierarchy. As pack leader, you can encourage the dogs to use non-aggressive means to define their status by giving preferential treatment to the dominant dog. This is typically, but not invariably, the first dog or the older dog. If you are not sure of the hierarchy, look for signs indicating that one dog defers to the other, such as stepping away from a toy or dish. The dominant dog may normally ignore the submissive dog, which is fine. Never force them to interact.
- Under no circumstances allow the dogs to establish their own dominance through aggression. In addition to the danger factor it will transmit a disastrous message. A genuine pack leader never tolerates this behavior between subordinates.
- If the dogs have already had aggressive incidents keep them on short leads when they interact so you can separate them quickly if needed. Always keep them separated when unsupervised.
- Be on the alert for body language that signals impending aggression. Be ready to step in and end any encounter before it erupts into actual combat.
- It's impossible for the dogs to fight all the time. Consistently reward non-aggressive behavior. For most of the day, the dogs will likely tolerate or ignore each other. Reinforce this whenever it occurs.
- Condition the dogs to relax on command in specific situations that regularly promote overexcitement and aggression, such as when you are preparing their dinner.

59

6 Choosing a Professional Trainer

Many owners perceive a professional trainer as a dog repairman. You take your malfunctioning Dachshund to the expert for a bit of tinkering and the training bugs are fixed. In reality, a good trainer will teach *you* how to properly use your training tools.

Training should become seamlessly incorporated into your Dachshund's daily routine. Reinforcing good behavior and responding to undesirable tendencies should be a reflex habit for you. A few owners have a natural aptitude for this, but most of us need as much practice as our Dachshunds.

If your skills are not fine tuned, your Dachshund will regard your efforts as nothing more than background static to be tuned out. Good training is in the details. To be an effective trainer you must

- Reward good behavior the second it starts to occur.
- Develop a sixth sense about spotting and interrupting unwanted behavior before it happens.
- Recognize when it's beneficial to vary a reward schedule.
- Know when to switch from food rewards to praise or a toy.
- Realize when it is time to demand more from your dog.

- Recognize that you may need to start over because the dog has become hopelessly confused by the training.

Very few of us have an innate ability to make these judgment calls without expert guidance. Rather than training your dog for you, a professional can help you perfect your skills. For example, an expert can help you learn to properly modulate your voice, use your body language and gestures effectively, avoid confusing your dog with contradictory or conflicting messages, avoid accidentally rewarding the wrong response, improve your timing, and decide when to use various techniques most effectively.

Choosing a Class or Trainer for Your Dachshund

Training classes are fairly easy to find in just about every mid-sized town or city. This doesn't imply that they are equally worthwhile. Professional certification is not required of dog trainers and anyone can print up business cards advertising their expertise. In addition, many trainers are not suited to working with Dachshunds and the wrong approach can result in more harm than good for your dog. Be prepared to encounter a tremendous range of proficiency and training philosophies as you explore your options. There are many qualities to look for, and just as many to avoid.

- Seek recommendations from other Dachshund owners in your area and do your own background research on various trainers.
- Keep in mind that accreditations from professional organizations may or may not be a valuable endorsement. Some groups have useful requirements for certification; others require nothing more than the completion of an application and the payment of a fee. None require practical testing to acquire certification.
- Sit in on a class and observe how the trainer responds to problem dogs. Winning awards, writing articles, or regularly dispensing online advice is no substitute for the actual training of dogs. Look for an instructor with substantial hands-on experience, especially with Dachshunds.
- On the other hand, a trainer with decades of experience is not a guaranteed match for you and your Dachshund. Some well-established trainers do not keep up-to-date with innovations in the field; others rigidly adhere to a single methodology, which may not work for a Dachshund. Trainers specializing in behavior issues often have a more flexible approach.
- If a trainer advertises as a behaviorist, ask about background and credentials in this area. Licensing is not required but the

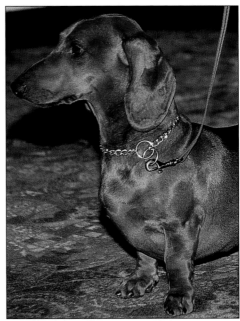

Every Dachshund can benefit from some formal training.

trainer should have practical experience justifying the claim. Academically trained behavior consultants should have credentials issued by the American College of Behaviorists or the Animal Behavior Society. Credentials should always be backed up with working experience.

- Most trainers advertise gentle humane methods. This sounds fine, but could mean anything. Every training technique includes discouraging unwanted behavior, ranging from a stern *NO*, to a jerk on the lead, to more forceful measures. Don't hesitate to ask about the nitty-gritty details of a trainer's methodology. Obviously you'll want to avoid trainers who employ harsh methods, but you need one who is willing and able to control the dogs.

Basic Training Classes

Beginner classes are generally group sessions that include dogs of all ages, sizes, and temperament, each accompanied by owners with varying abilities to manage them. The class should be run by an expert trainer able to sustain a calm, stable atmosphere that is conducive to learning. Dachshunds are highly sensitive and responsive to their surroundings under the best of circumstances so don't even consider enrolling your dog in a poorly controlled class. Doing so will make it impossible for your dog to learn anything, and may undo all the work you've already done to instill confidence, focus, and attention.

The class size should be small, with a maximum of 10 dog/owner teams per class. Larger classes should have additional instructors or class monitors on hand. Some classes group dogs by size or restrict enrollment to large or small dogs, a helpful, but not always available, option.

The presence of unmanageable, aggressive, or hyperactive dogs can put your Dachshund on the defensive for the entire class, precluding the chance of learning anything. If necessary, the instructor should step in and provide solutions to help owners maintain control of their dogs. This may be as simple as switching a dog's collar and lead or moving some dogs to different parts of the room. It may also indicate that a particular dog is not suited to a group class.

A good trainer watches continually for indications of problems between dogs in the class and intervenes before they escalate. Owners may not realize that their dog's behavior is verging on disorderly or dangerous. It is the instructor's responsibility to recognize these warning signs and step in before the behavior interferes with other dogs in the class. The instructor should also be aware of each dog's ability to cope with the classroom environment and should be able to recognize the causes of problem behavior.

Unless the class is one geared solely toward puppy socialization, playing and socializing between dogs should not be encouraged. If the dogs start perceiving the class as one long, happy play date, maintaining their attention becomes an ongoing battle. Dachshunds require encouragement to remain handler oriented. This should be incorporated into the class structure.

Learning to tolerate distractions is part of the training process, but a tense or chaotic atmosphere will defeat the purpose. There should be ample space between each dog/owner team to allow them to practice each exercise without interference from other dogs. Typically, the instructor describes, then demonstrates, each new exercise and observes as the students try putting it into practice. The class size should allow individualized time to ensure that every student completely understands each new technique as it is presented.

You should also have opportunities to ask questions and seek advice on specific training problems. For instance, if your Dachshund is not responding to a particular method, a good trainer will try a different approach or show you what you may be doing wrong. If your dog fails to respond to a training technique after three attempts, don't persist in a futile attempt to make it work. Try something different. This is essential for a quirky breed like the Dachshund.

You should be able to see that your Dachshund is benefiting from the class. A little apprehension at first is to be expected, but this reaction should disappear by the second class. Your dog should arrive happy, enjoy the work, and behave calmly when you get home. If instead, you notice your Dachshund becoming nervous, defensive, or withdrawn from the experience, something is wrong. Discuss the problem with the instructor and don't hesitate to drop out and find a different class if you feel that is best for your dog.

Could be an itch ... or an anxiety attack.

Puppy Kindergarten

New owners are usually encouraged to enroll their puppy in a class for socialization and an introduction to training basics. This seems like a very simple training format. However, the tone of this class can have a lifelong impact on your Dachshund's developing personality, providing unparalleled opportunities for learning and socialization in a controlled environment, supervised by experts.

Puppy kindergarten can be beneficial for both puppies *and* their owners. A good program provides an experiential base for dogs and handlers to learn handling and communication skills and helps define a game plan for future training. In addition the class may draw attention to potential behavior issues early on, provid-

ing owners with a base to draw should problems erupt later. For example, if your Dachshund is somewhat hesitant and aloof, a skilled trainer can design a program to revise these tendencies before your fearful puppy gets into the habit of relying on coping mechanisms such as defensive aggression.

Puppy kindergarten programs can take many forms. Beware of those that attempt to treat puppies like miniature adult dogs. Puppies do not have the stamina, confidence, or attention span to cope with a structured training class. At best, it will be a waste of time. At worst it will seriously undermine your Dachshund's interest in training. Lessons should be short, positive, and interspaced with plenty of play.

On the other hand, you don't want too much play. Classes that function as playgroups do little more than provide puppies with playmates. Making dog-to-dog socialization the focus of the class imparts the

Training Tip: Pay Attention

If you have trouble maintaining your Dachshund's focus in class, stress, not simple inattentiveness, may be the cause. Watch for the following behaviors.

■ *Constant yawning, lip licking, ear scratching, or floor sniffing are displacement activities meant to alleviate anxiety.*

■ *A nervous dog may persistently scan the environment in worried manner or overreact to surprises such as a new dog walking into class.*

■ *Constant whining or barking may be your Dachshund's way of relieving the stress and insecurity he feels in a large group of dogs.*

human leadership, dog skills, and the understanding of canine social structure. None of this will be possible unless the instructor is highly proficient in concepts of dog behavior.

Family Dog Training

In the past, the majority of training classes consisted of eight weeks of regimented basic obedience. This continues to be the mainstay of dog training but many of these programs have been revised to address the real needs of dog owners. They have evolved into an extension of progressive puppy kindergarten classes, providing owners with skills for good dog management. Although the majority of the focus is on teaching basic commands, these classes also emphasize the behavioral aspects of training, helping owners to better understand their dogs. This is sometimes described as situational training. For Dachshunds, classes like this are invaluable.

Your Dachshund's mastery of *sit* or *stay* in a classroom setting provides no real-life solution to everyday canine behavior issues. A good family dog class can give you the tools to successfully manage problems like barking at the postman or jumping on guests. One of the most important aspects of these classes is making owners aware of unintentional training that encourages problem behavior. Jumping, for instance, is a classic example of canine attention-seeking behavior. Owners may not care for this type of greeting, but it makes perfect sense to the dog. The behavior is often reinforced because owners have been advised to use traditional training methods that often have little

message that human interaction plays a secondary role in your Dachshund's socialization. Especially for this breed, that approach can be a significant waste of critical time in your puppy's socialization period. Equally damaging are classes structured to allow dogs to work out their own hierarchical issues. Not only can this be dangerous, it also totally diminishes the role of human leadership. Assertive dogs will remain assertive and defensive dogs will resort to defensive behavior. If your dog has a tendency to become excitable in the presence of other dogs, this atmosphere will only encourage it more. It will also teach your young Dachshund to resist any boundaries you impose.

Look for a class that focuses on socializing puppies to become handler-oriented within a high-density dog environment. It should provide a balanced emphasis on

Training Tip

Many owners are cautioned by their veterinarians to postpone training until their pup's vaccinations are complete. Some puppies will do well in spite of this, some will not.

For most Dachshunds, this is not a good approach. Intensive, rather than random socialization is essential. Neglecting behavior issues in favor of a concern for health safety becomes a dubious trade-off for both puppy and owner. With expert guidance, both issues can be successfully managed to insure minimal health risk and timely exposure to the world.

Puppy kindergarten can provide unparalleled socialization opportunities.

effect on Dachshunds. You may have been told to teach your dog to sit rather than to jump up to greet you, but the concept of sitting down when the urge to jump takes over is not likely to make any sense to a Dachshund. Likewise, ignoring or restraining the dog in response to jumping often simply escalates the excitability that triggered the jumping in the first place. The real solution involves helping the dog take responsibility and make a decision to choose an alternate response. This type of class will make it much easier for you to evaluate your dog's responses and employ the right tools to make training work.

Advanced Training Classes

Individual techniques, training philosophies, and classroom atmosphere take on a far greater significance at advanced levels of training. At this stage, you must become very picky about the instructors you choose to work with. Don't be overly impressed or intimidated by a person's background. Most trainers at this level have a successful track record as competitors. Phenomenal success training Poodles or Shelties does not imply equal skill when working with Dachshunds. Be skeptical of trainers that make big promises about what your dog will accomplish in the show ring.

Both you and your Dachshund must establish a good working relationship with this person. Trust and communication should be your first priorities.

Obedience

For Dachshunds, advanced obedience training represents a formidable challenge.

an internal sense of satisfaction about the behavior. Praise and food rewards will achieve cooperation for a while, but these are merely stepping stones to willing compliance. Ultimately, the dog should internalize his response to training and perceive the teamwork itself as rewarding. This is accomplished through consistently positive cause-and-effect experiences.

Look for a program that utilizes a combination of techniques. Rigid methodology or a single approach to training is not likely to encourage a Dachshund's natural desire to figure things out. Learning and obedience are two different things. Your training methods must help the dog understand what is wanted and what is not. Only when your Dachshund learns to take responsibility for training responses will they become self-regulating.

Agility

Exciting, challenging, and equally fun for spectators and participants, it's easy to understand why agility is so popular. Because of this, classes are easy to find. As is the case for every type of training, finding the right class is critical for your Dachshund.

A good agility class can do wonders for many aspects of your Dachshund's training:

Discouraging your Dachshund from jumping up may require a less conventional approach to the problem.

While many dog sports are based on training that is essentially self-motivating (tracking and field trial work, for instance, appeal to a Dachshund's natural predatory instinct), obedience training is not innately rewarding. If you hope to make your Dachshund a reliable obedience competitor, you must focus on instilling an internal reward mechanism. This requires a balanced approach that encourages the dog to take responsibility for choices, rather than forcing compliance. Bribing or forcing a dog to obey commands will never create

- Foster a sense of teamwork with your dog.
- Instill a positive attitude.
- Help the dog learn to cope with distractions.
- Channel excess energy.
- Build confidence.

All these potential advantages make it tempting to dive in without thoroughly investigating the possibilities. That can be a mistake. Agility work is performed off lead, and focus and control are essential. This highly stimulating environment is not ideal for every dog with strong predatory instinct. If your Dachshund tends to be highly reactive, hyper-vigilant, or have trouble maintaining focus around other dogs, you'll run into problems in a poorly managed class. The instructor must be able to ensure the safety of small dogs in the classroom and be able to keep every dog's arousal levels within safe limits.

Because agility is usually so much fun for dogs, it's also easy for an inexperienced handler to push their dog too far too fast. Dachshunds are not noted for their natural caution. It's an instructor's responsibility to keep you mindful of the physical challenges and gauge your dog's ability.

Dachshunds can do great in obedience but they don't always respond to traditional methods.

Conformation

Training your Dachshund to succeed in the conformation ring poses challenges on several levels. Watching from ringside, the entire process looks deceptively easy. Conformation judging is designed as an objective means of evaluating physical structure, temperament, and breed-specific traits. Each entrant is assessed by comparing the physical attributes of the dog to the description in its official breed standard of perfection. In reality, no dog exists that can match this ideal and showmanship plays a big role in making a winning impression.

Show dogs must be confident extroverts, with an instinctively ability to focus on their handler, respond to the judge, and ignore their environment. Training a Dachshund to do things effortlessly is

often a protracted endeavor requiring infinite patience. Your job is to enhance your dog's performance while making this contribution seem effortless—something that requires perfect teamwork between dog and handler. Be prepared for a lot of work to properly present your Dachshund. Unprepared for the challenges and commitment necessary to succeed, the typical novice remains in this sport for only five to seven years.

Choosing the right dog is equally important. In addition to conforming to breed type and possessing sound structure, a show dog must have mental and physical stamina. The ability to manage stress is party genetic and partly learned. Genetic aspects of temperament should be considered when selecting a show puppy and conditioning and training to instill mental

Your Dachshund should be very reliable off lead before you try agility training.

resiliency is a crucial part of raising a show dog. Your puppy must learn to accept variations in routine and plenty of attention from strangers. It may be impossible to convince a Dachshund to enjoy these things without an early positive introduction.

Serious exhibitors begin socializing and training show prospects when they are just a few weeks old. Daily routine training at home should emphasize basics such as learning to tolerate examination and walking confidently on lead. By four months of age your puppy should be enrolled in a conformation class. Training classes will help both of you become acquainted with aspects of the show routine and learn to concentrate despite distractions. If you are new to the sport it is essential to find an instructor who understands a Dachshund's environmental sensitivity and emotional

quirks. The training experience should suit your puppy's maturity level and nurture confidence. Pushing a puppy into regimented training too fast can cause boredom or disinterest. Once this happens, it can be difficult to fix. Experienced trainers concur that it is very hard to rekindle show spirit in a Dachshund.

Puppies become eligible to compete in conformation shows at six months of age. A knowledgeable instructor can help you decide if your puppy is mentally and physically ready for competition at that age. Match shows can be a less stressful alternative to help novice handlers and puppies prepare for the show ring. Don't underestimate the value of these practice runs. No matter how well you perform at home or at class, competing in public is a whole different ball game.

7 *Teaching Basic Commands*

The Goal of Basic Commands

Every dog should know *come*, *sit*, *stay*, *down*, and *heel*, but training is not about the mechanics of a perfect response to commands. Your primary goal is to establish a baseline of responsiveness from your Dachshund in all situations. A reliable response to these commands lays a foundation that will prove useful in countless situations. The process of teaching them also provides invaluable insight into your Dachshund's personality, making it easier for you to choose the right tool to make training work.

Formal Training

Even if your Dachshund is a young puppy, it's never too early to start working on basic commands. Two ten-minute training sessions per day are plenty. Keep them shorter if you are still building your Dachshund's motivation. Short lessons also make it easier for you to remain focused when working with your dog. It is more important to concentrate on how your dog is responding, rather than the immediate results of the exercise. Your tone

and pace should be geared to build motivation, but never overwhelm or confuse the dog.

House Rules

The rules of the house should be taught at the same time as basic commands. You will be using commands to help your Dachshund understand boundaries and choose desirable behavior responses. This combined approach helps you formulate practical solutions that work for your dog in your environment.

Rules of Play

Playing is the motivation for much of a puppy's social interaction with both dogs and humans. Canine/human play demands an especially complex repertoire of skills, self-control, and sensitivity to participate in complicated rituals with another species. Interactive play with your puppy fosters trust and communication and provides reassurance about her status in the pack.

As they mature, puppies begin to incorporate adult interests into their play, such as pack order and territorial defense. They may also attempt to assert dominance

Training Tip

If after three attempts a particular approach is not getting any results, try something different such as breaking the exercise into smaller components, using a different reward, a new vocal cue or gesture, or working in a different environment. And consider the following:

- *Is the dog losing focus due to confusion, stress, or boredom?*
- *Are you reinforcing the right response by timing your commands and reinforcements appropriately?*

As you gradually figure out why the approach is not working, you can apply your discoveries to other aspects of training in order to streamline your methods.

during play with humans. This is a normal facet of canine mentality: from a dog's viewpoint, social behaviors such as play are a mechanism for improving one's status. Through playful exchanges with adult dogs, puppies experiment with behavior boundaries, while avoiding actual confrontation. They use the same approach with humans. It's important to remember however, that puppies have a short attention span and often revise their intentions in the midst of a play session. Play can morph into aggression, directed toward perceived threats to territory or status. If you fail to react appropriately, you'll send a message that it's okay to challenge human members of their pack.

Take tug of war for instance. It is a favorite game between dogs and most

enjoy it just as much with a human playmate. This seemingly innocent game, however, is often cited as a trigger for aggressive behavior. Two dogs will abruptly end a game that escalates beyond acceptable limits; when faced with the same situation, humans can exhibit contradictory reactions.

As pack leader it is your responsibility to direct play appropriately. You should be the one to initiate games, not your dog. This gets your Dachshund into the habit of shifting in and out of prey drive and emphasizes your status as leader. Your Dachshund's play sessions should be limited to specific times and places chosen by you, such as a play room or backyard. You should also control access to toys. For this to be meaningful, all family members must reinforce this training. When it's playtime bring the toys out and put them away when you decide playtime is over. If your Dachshund accidentally nips or becomes too wild during play, call a time out. Barking, pushing, jumping, or nipping to get your attention or demand play should not be tolerated. Your Dachshund should understand that it is not okay to bother you when you are working or trying to cook dinner. This part of training should include a special command to let your dog know when it is time to settle down and leave you alone. This is especially important if you have multiple dogs that are likely to engage in rowdy free-for-all play sessions in the house.

No Barking

Excessive barking is a common Dachshund problem that is far easier to prevent than

Training Tip

Some Dachshunds can be nippy when playing or taking treats from your hand. Dogs have the ability to fine-tune their bite pressure but this habit is learned. Regardless of the circumstances, nipping should be firmly discouraged every time it happens.

Teach your Dachshund to politely take something from your hand. Approach your dog with a hand full of treats in your closed fist. Bring them right up to the dog's nose and present the treats. If your Dachshund grabs for your hand, close it and correct the dog with an "ah ah." Do this repeatedly until the dog responds in some way that is neutral and polite. At that point, reward the dog with praise and a treat from your other hand. If your Dachshund is already a confirmed food shark, it may take three or four weeks of practice to discourage this grabby attitude about food.

Some dogs will take a treat gently from your hand, while others require some training to learn this concept.

pack leader is eroded. Excess energy and attention-seeking behavior can be redirected but that is not going to happen without your participation.

Leash Training

Leash training is a good precursor to basic commands. It helps you establish leadership and control both indoors and out.

Since dogs accept new experiences more readily before four months of age, this is the best time to introduce your pup to leash training. First introductions are more easily managed when the pup is tired and relaxed after eating or playing. Hold the collar or harness open with a treat in the other hand and encourage the pup to approach. Use a special command and provide a treat when putting it on the puppy to instill a positive association about the

to remedy. If your Dachshund barks at you to get your attention and direct your behavior, you are not being a very good pack leader. Every time you respond to this sort of thing, it is reinforced and it will escalate.

If you want your dog to be calm and quiet at home it's up to you to insist on more subtle forms of communication. Respond with the *relax* command, rather than tolerating the noise. This also reinforces your house rules. Every time your dog demands attention or becomes overexcited in your presence, your role as the

Home Schooling

Collars

A properly fitting collar or harness is essential for comfort, safety, and control. Collars should be positioned high on the neck right under the jaw. A collar that slips down the dog's neck will cause discomfort and choking as the dog pulls against it. A properly positioned collar makes it easy to control the dog's head and ensure that the dog is paying attention to you

Buckle Collar

Buckle collars are usually made of nylon webbing or leather, with a buckle similar to a belt buckle, or with a quick release buckle. To test for proper fit, you should be able to slip two fingers under the collar. Test to ensure the dog cannot pull the collar off. Narrow-headed breeds like Dachshunds are quite adept at this.

Slip Collar

Slip collars consist of a length of chain or nylon rope with rings at either end. The chain is pulled through the ring at one end to form a loop around the dog's neck. This type of collar should be approximately four inches larger than the circumference of the dog's neck. This design is more secure than a buckle collar because it will tighten if the dog pulls. Put it on the right way to ensure that it instantly loosens when pressure is released.

Martingale

Martingale collars have two loops: the smaller loop is called the "control loop."

Proper fit is essential for comfort and safety.

Slip collar

does not encircle the throat is more comfortable than other styles. Dogs can pull out of any style harness if it is not correctly fitted. Estimate size by measuring around the widest part of the chest behind the elbows and adding two inches. Try the harness on your Dachshund to check for secure fit and unrestricted movement before using it outdoors.

This loop is attached to the leash and tightens when it is pulled. The second loop is the "adjustment loop." This loop is used to adjust the size of the collar to fit your dog. This lead-and-collar combination tightens in response to pulling and loosens automatically. These collars are quite safe and escape-proof.

Harness

Many dogs accept a harness more readily than a collar but it doesn't provide the same control. Most dogs instinctively pull in response to restraint and a harness can exacerbate this. A step-in harness that

No matter which type of collar your dog wears, it should be positioned right under the jaw for maximum comfort and control.

Leads

A six-foot nylon or leather lead is safer and provides far better control than a flex lead. The clip should be securely designed. The most common types are the thumb spring latch and lobster claw, both of which can open accidentally. Carbine or cross-over thumb release latches are more secure.

Training Tip: The House Leash

Once your Dachshund is leash trained you have the option of using a house leash, a short leash used indoors. This is a great tool for retraining an adult, habituating a puppy, or interrupting bad behavior. It can be especially helpful in situations where you have trouble calming your dog, such as when you arrive home or start preparing dinner.

You don't need to hold the leash all the time, but it is there when you need to and the dog is always aware of it. "No" does not always mean "no" in the world of Dachshunds. You can grab the leash to interrupt bad behavior or stop the dog from running off and ignoring a command. Your Dachshund will be well aware of the fact that you have the ability to follow through with commands, so ignoring you is no longer an option.

After a week or two, your Dachshund will have a new outlook concerning your leadership role.

experience. Leave the collar for a couple of hours and give the pup a chew toy for distraction. After three days of this acclimation process, attach the leash and encourage the pup to follow you for a few steps. Don't stint on the reinforcements at this stage. Leash training requires variable amounts of time and patience. Pulling, jerking, or dragging the pup creates a negative association

If possible, introduce your puppy to the lead and collar by four months of age.

and encourages the instinct to pull away. A sensitive touch with this training tool can prevent a multitude of problems associated with walking on lead.

As soon as your Dachshund accepts the lead, begin to reinforce the idea of walking at your side without pulling or lagging. Encourage the pup to match your pace on a loose lead. Keep the leash short enough to prevent the puppy from getting tangled but loose enough for comfort. Work in an area free from distractions and generously reward every attempt to walk at the correct pace. Varying your pace and making unpredictable turns helps to discourage the pup from straying from your side. If the pup does lunge ahead or lag behind, use treats, small vocal corrections, and light tugs on the lead to put a stop to it immediately. Use a light touch; too many corrections can trigger an avoidance response or teach your Dachshund to ignore you altogether.

Wait until the pup is confident walking on the lead at your side before adding distractions to the training sessions. Outdoor distractions are often enough to ensure that a Dachshund forgets about the leash. Of course, depending on your pup's personality, this may complicate or facilitate the training process. It's helpful to use two different commands to let your Dachshund know when to remain close by your side and when it's okay to wander out at the end of the lead—this should never include pulling or lunging.

If you are lead training an older Dachshund, use the same approach but prepare for somewhat slower progress. It may help to first teach the dog to walk at your side without a leash, either indoors or in a fenced yard. Once the dog is comfortable with this, attach the leash and repeat the exercises for several days before venturing out on the street.

Sit, Stay, Down, *and* Come

Begin every lesson with the *pay attention* or *relax* command to ensure that your dog is in the proper frame of mind. Eye contact is key to establishing and maintaining communication, which is essential to the learning process. Dachshunds respond on a scale of 0–10 depending on your actual control of the situation.

■ During training, narrow your dog's range of options through a combination of control, correction, and reward.

■ Never give a command you are not prepared to enforce. This is especially important when introducing something new. It won't take much for your dog to figure out that disobeying or ignoring you pays off.

■ Work in an environment where you can control the outcome and ensure the response you want. Train indoors or in a small fenced area, or keep the dog on lead.

■ After giving a command, watch your Dachshund's body language and use shaping to reinforce a response or manage the situation by intervening. For instance, if the dog is on the verge of breaking a *stay* command give a verbal correction like *ah ah* before it happens. If your Dachshund starts to comply with a *sit* or *down* command, shape that response with positive reinforcement.

When you are sure your Dachshund understands and responds reliably to a command, gradually add challenges to the situation. Don't be tempted to proceed too fast. Your Dachshund may have mastered coming when called in the controlled setting of a training class, but may refuse to return when off lead at the dog park, where you have virtually no control. Your dog will be excited, distracted, and perfectly capable of outrunning you. You, in turn will become increasingly angry, frustrated, and embarrassed.

Putting yourself and your dog in situations that you can't control effectively de-condition your Dachshund to the training you have instilled. Yelling, threatening, chasing, or grabbing the dog will not get your message across, but will intensify the unraveling of the training process. (It's also bad for your blood pressure.) Your Dachshund may decide that avoiding you or ignoring you is a preferable alternative.

Sit

With your Dachshund on a leash give the *pay attention* command and show the dog a treat in your hand. Bring the treat near the dog's nose and slowly move it over the dog's head. Thanks to the way they are built, most Dachshunds will automatically

Hold the treat slightly above your dog's head to lure him into a sit position.

Training Do's And Don'ts

- *Do enforce consistent rules in a calm, controlled, and patient manner.*
- *Do use simple, consistent phrases when giving commands.*
- *Do train in a controlled setting, relatively free of distractions.*
- *Do calmly, firmly reinforce commands if the dog doesn't comply.*
- *Don't be stingy with rewards. Give at least one treat every three seconds at first.*
- *Do constantly reinforce control with praise.*
- *Don't add distractions and temptations to the training process too quickly. Instead introduce them as the dog's ability improves.*
- *Don't repeat the same command over and over. Doing so teaches your dog that persistence pays off. Deciding if or when to respond is not the dog's decision.*
- *Don't whine, nag, or use your dog's name in negative context during training.*
- *Do use your dog's name when giving an active command, such as come, but don't use it to reinforce a passive command, such as stay.*

---

sit as their head moves up and back to follow your hand. Pushing your dog into a sit position is more likely to elicit the opposite response. Reward anything resembling a sit. If the dog tries to grab the treat, correct this with an *ah ah* and start again. Continue rewarding every response that is remotely correct.

A clicker or hand gesture can help shape and reinforce the response but don't add a verbal cue until the dog understands the exercise. Until the dog understands what you want her to do, verbal commands are more apt to confuse than reinforce.

Stay

Once your Dachshund has mastered *sit*, it is not difficult to segue into *stay*. Begin with the same sequence. With your Dachshund on a leash, give the *pay attention* command and use a treat to lure the dog next to your side. Follow this with a *sit* command. When the dog is sitting, wait a second or two before giving a release command and a reward. Your dog will normally turn to face you after getting up, which gives you the opportunity to make eye contact and maintain control. This little maneuver becomes more important when you start adding distractions to the exercise or working without the leash.

If you notice that your dog is about to break from the *stay* position, interrupt before the dog can follow through. At first, don't expect your Dachshund to remain in place for more than a few seconds. You can combine the exercise with a hand signal but don't add a verbal cue too early in the training process. Many dogs misunderstand and instinctively get up rather than stay put in response to a verbal cue.

When the dog grasps the idea of sitting and remaining in place add more time to the routine and alternate long and short *sit, stay* exercises. The next step is to gradually move a few inches away from the dog. Don't be tempted to work too fast. Pay attention to your dog's progress and increase the reward schedule if necessary.

Do not combine *stay* and *come* commands. Use a different word to release the dog from a *stay*. Otherwise the dog may decide that *stay* and *come* are equally acceptable options in that situation. To a Dachshund, that will make perfect sense.

Ignoring distractions can be the biggest challenge for a Dachshund. Work on this part of the exercise last, after you have successfully added time and distance to the command. At first, when adding distractions, reinforce the training by decreasing the length of the *stay*, working closer to the dog, and upping the reward schedule. Expecting too much from your Dachshund too soon can completely undermine the work you have done so far. You must give the dog sufficient time to internalize a response that is totally contrary to normal Dachshund behavior.

Come

The challenge of teaching your Dachshund to stay pales in comparison to teaching her to *come* when called. Some Dachshunds will never reliably come back when the leash comes off. The right approach is crucial to instilling a reliable recall. If your Dachshund is already in the habit of ignoring you, start by revising your training procedure, including a new command. This is one command that must have a verbal cue attached, so if your Dachshund has already learned to ignore it, start fresh. Hand signals can help to reinforce the idea but are useless in many situations where coming when called is essential.

Start teaching *come* with your Dachshund on a long lead. Walk backwards, encouraging the dog to follow you. If the dog ignores you give the *look* command and a slight tug on the lead. As soon as the dog starts moving towards you reinforce this with a clicker, praise, body language, and treats. It's also helpful to give the command when your dog is already heading in your direction. This is something you should reinforce throughout the day, such as at mealtimes, to instill a positive association.

The leash ensures that your Dachshund does not have the option of ignoring you, but your goal is to have the dog come reliably when off lead. This should be part of the process from the start. Work in a small area so you can take the dog by the collar and reinforce the command if necessary. This must always be done in a positive manner with praise and treats. Indoors, the exercise can be turned into a game. Two or more people can alternately call the dog from room to room, supplying plenty of encouragement and rewards.

Targeting is another helpful tool in recall training. Providing something to focus on can keep your Dachshund reliably heading your way rather than taking a detour to a tempting distraction. Reliably instilling this response in your Dachshund can require quite a bit of effort. Don't sabotage your training.

■ Don't let the dog ignore the command.
■ Never ask your Dachshund to come to you if you are angry or planning to do something the dog dislikes, such as nail clipping.
■ Keep your reward schedule geared to the dog's response level. For some Dachshunds this can mean repeatedly backtracking to a higher reward rate.
■ Constantly reinforce the command in varied situations using varied rewards.

Down

With Dachshunds, it is important to work slowly and patiently teaching the *down* command. Dogs are reluctant to lie down or stay down if they are aroused or fearful. Lure the dog into position and gradually shape the response. Using your hand or the leash to force the dog into position may get results in the short run, but will never produce a reliable response.

Begin with your Dachshund standing, facing you, and paying attention. To ease strain on your back, sit or kneel in front of the dog. Hold a treat close to the dog's nose and slowly move it to the dog's feet. As the dog's head follows, the body will lean back, which is a slight approximation of what you are seeking. Keep the treat on the floor under your hand, as close as possible to the dog's paws. This makes it difficult for the dog to get it without lying down. Of course, Dachshunds are built for challenges like this and a bit of creativity may be required. A variety of methods will achieve results as long as the dog is allowed to figure out what you want and comply voluntarily.

■ Positioning the dog on a mat or dog bed may encourage the idea of lying down.
■ For some dogs a slick surface puts gravity into the equation helping the dog slide into position.
■ Try sitting on the floor and positioning the dog underneath your bent knee.
■ Put your Dachshund on a chair or table while you sit on the floor holding your food lure slightly below the dog's level.

Use praise, treats, or your clicker to shape the response by rewarding every

"Shake hands" can be reinforced with a treat.

move in the right direction. A gesture of sweeping your hand downward towards the dog's feet can help reinforce the idea, but do not add a verbal command until your dog understands the exercise.

Tricks

Tricks may seem superfluous compared to more important aspects of training, but they can be just as effective as a behavior management tool. They also represent a nice change of pace from regular training. Once they have a couple of tricks under their belt, most dogs enjoy showing them off.

Shake Hands

Shake hands is the classic dog trick and a good way to redirect jumping on guests into a charming greeting. Since many dogs instinctively lift a paw to get attention, it's also fairly easy to teach. If your dog has a habit of doing this, reinforce it with a well-timed click or treat. If not, teach in a systematic fashion by putting your Dachshund into a *sit/stay* and gently cupping your hand under one front paw. As the dog lifts this paw, click and reward. After a few tries this should begin to happen on cue. Shape the response with praise and treats. As the dog's response becomes more reliable, begin holding your hand in front of the dog rather than reaching for the paw, and add the command *shake hands*. To really impress your friends, use the same procedure to teach your Dachshund to alternately shake hands with the right or left paw on command.

The Balancing Act

A Dachshund's long muzzle is perfect for balancing a treat. This trick is a great way to reinforce impulse control and focus, discourage food grabbing, and impress party guests. Balance a treat on your dog's muzzle while using your other hand to support the dog's head under the jaw. Use eye contact and the relax command to encourage your dog to keep still. After a few seconds remove your support hand and give a release command along with the treat. After a few successful attempts remove the support hand and wait two seconds before giving the release command and the reward. Your Dachshund will soon realize that the treat is forthcoming. Gradually extend the time and stop using your hand to keep the dog's head still.

8 Common Training Mistakes

Early Warning Signs of Training and Behavior Problems

It's sometimes tricky to spot subtle indications of a budding behavior problem, especially in a puppy. The old adage, "forgive and forget," describes the way most of us tend to raise a puppy. Most of the time, this is a fine approach, but it can cause you to overlook serious behavior issues. By the time you realize that something is wrong, the problem may have progressed to an unmanageable stage. Some puppies may well be accidents waiting to happen, but this is not simply a matter of fate. Personality traits evolve as a combination of innate predisposition, learning, and environment.

An unstable temperament may not become evident until adolescence or adulthood, but it is possible to identify significant behavior traits between 8 to 16 weeks. Excitability, defensive behavior (both avoidance and aggression), opportunistic rank enhancement, resource guarding, and attachment issues are often evident early on. The emotional centers of a puppy's brain are open to influence during these weeks, and unbalanced personality traits can be revised through tailored training. However, recognizing personality quirks may require professional behavior evaluation.

A skilled trainer can tell you if your puppy's behavior is understandable, acceptable, or aberrant. Problem behavior in Dachshund puppies usually falls into specific categories.

Resource Guarding

Resource issues such as food and object possession and/or guarding access to desired locations are often overlooked in puppy training. Through their early experiences competing with their littermates, puppies are conditioned to take what they want and guard it with all their might. From the canine perspective, resources are not meant to be shared.

In a human environment dogs are expected to be cooperative and subordinate, accepting the idea that humans have first access to resources. This is a difficult concept for puppies to grasp under the best of circumstances. They can easily develop habits like stealing food, guarding objects, defending favorite sleeping spots, or behaving protectively toward a favorite

Puppies love their toys, but this can evolve into the undesirable habit of resource guarding.

person. Although the resulting aggression may seem to come out of nowhere, these behaviors do not happen suddenly. If you are paying attention, they can be effectively revised at an early stage.

Predatory Behavior

Puppies often begin exhibiting predatory behavior by eight weeks of age. Early exposure or participation encourages and intensifies its expression. Puppies can learn to moderate this instinctive response, but success is more likely if you start early. Wait too long and it may evolve into predatory aggression or compulsive behavior such as barking, digging, or hyperactivity meant to relive anxiety or frustration.

Inadequate Social Skills

Without ongoing socialization, dominant or submissive personality traits can become extreme. Many puppies possess dominant or submissive tendencies but their personalities remain within the bounds of normal behavior due to a combination of early training and socialization. Those raised in a commercial environment may not receive adequate human or canine interaction to curb extreme tendencies. The end result is a puppy incapable of moderate responses.

Some puppies inherit a passive personality; others resort to a submissive strategy to avoid confrontation. Either way, it can become a life sentence unless the puppy is encouraged to develop social and communication skills. After the closure of a puppy's imprinting phase, behavior modification can help, but will never entirely correct, the problem.

A rude, pushy, dominant puppy's behavior can also be due to insufficient early learning opportunities. Puppies must learn how to appropriately initiate interactions and deflect aggression. Socially inept puppies often score well on temperament tests but they remain prime candidates for dysfunctional and possibly dangerous behavior sometimes bordering on sociopathic. Their limited social skills make it impossible for them to utilize strategies other than fight or flight. They remain capable of improving their social skills, optimally before four months of age, if given opportunities to interact with well-socialized adult dogs.

Understanding Behavior Problems

Behavior problems are easier to identify in adult dogs, but that doesn't provide any clues into the underlying reasons. Mistakes by handlers and the dog's state of physical and mental health can all impact behavior.

Handler Errors

Miscommunication

Misinterpreting or dismissing the importance of your Dachshund's communication signals accounts for many training problems. Even the most straightforward canine signals can be misunderstood if you fail to pay attention or inject your own interpretation into the equation. Our effortless ability to generalize can also make it hard to understand a dog's perceptions. Dachshunds possess an excellent ability to discriminate between small details but don't automatically look at the big picture. If they do look at the big picture it may be quite different from yours.

Unintentional Training

Dachshunds are experts at making connections between unrelated events. This can occur actively, in response to training, or randomly, through their natural opportunistic efforts to exploit their environment. Just as they learn to ignore irrelevant details, they zero in on the important ones. This is sometimes referred to as "fast mapping," the ability to grasp connections between unrelated ideas. You may not be aware of them, but these learned associations can yield a payoff or create a groundless fear.

Nagging

Your approach to communication may inadvertently condition your Dachshund to ignore you. Don't confuse the dog with contradictory or overlapping commands. Repeating commands without following through will reinforce the idea that it is okay to ignore you. Likewise, be aware of inappropriate reprimands or negative reinforcements such as constantly repeating the dog's name as a form of scolding. The dog will eventually become desensitized and tune you out or resort to avoidance.

Improper Timing

Because Dachshunds are quite sensitive and emotional, inconsistent, poorly timed reinforcements or corrections can completely derail training. A poorly timed correction will confuse the dog by admonishing the wrong action. If this happens repeatedly, the dog will try to draw some kind of conclusion from the events and start avoiding something, but probably not what you had in mind. If the dog becomes sufficiently frustrated and confused, avoidance and anxiety may foster secondary behavior problems.

Mental or Physical Causes

Teething
Deciduous, or milk teeth, usually erupt between 15–26 days of age and can have a big impact on your puppy's behavior. Small breeds often begin teething later than large breeds. Females usually start teething earlier than male littermates and summer puppies start cutting their teeth earlier than winter puppies. The process normally coincides with weaning and a puppy's growing independence as the socialization period begins. However, puppies remain vulnerable and emotionally dependent on their dam during these weeks.

The second phase of teething commences around four months of age and can also be associated with behavior changes ranging from apathy to destructiveness. Males are especially prone to personality upsets because teething can coincide with adolescent hormonal surges, resulting in an unhappy combination of juvenile crankiness and adolescent bravado. Their attention span grows short and they may have difficulty concentrating. Although these

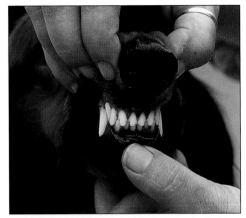

Examine your puppy's mouth frequently during the teething period. This will prevent a tendency to become "mouth shy."

issues are temporary, they can become long-term behavior problems if improperly managed.

It might be advisable to temporarily modify or curtail regular training; for instance, leash training can create a fear of the leash and collar if a puppy is suffering from mouth or jaw pain.

Adolescent Social Anxiety
Genetically programmed breed tendencies also begin to emerge or intensify during adolescence. The effects may be less pronounced in neutered animals, but they remain inseparable from breed type. Dachshunds may become less mindful of social cues as they become focused on hunting and automatically block out distractions.

A puppy's pheromone levels signal impending maturity long before physical changes become evident. This not only triggers physiological and behavioral changes,

83

Some puppies become noticeably shy during adolescence.

but also strongly impacts a puppy's social status. Other dogs begin perceiving them as competitors, rather than juveniles, subjecting them to canine social pressures. Because the pack represents such an overwhelming source of security, this can also become a focal point of anxiety during adolescence. Pack hierarchy can effectively preserve peace but an adolescent may become subjected to routine bullying in multiple dog households. The resulting reaction can sometimes be mistaken for shyness or avoidance behavior as a puppy matures. It is important to be aware of canine power struggles or mild-mannered puppies may become seriously intimidated.

Testosterone production peaks when puppies are about ten months old—at levels nearly five times higher than an adult. The adrenal gland produces testosterone

in both sexes and even well-socialized puppies may experience a resultant degree of mental instability between six and twelve months. They may attempt to challenge their pack status by ignoring commands, inciting slight altercations with other dogs, guarding valued items, or engaging in territorial leg lifting. Some Dachshunds become standoffish at this age as hormones exacerbate natural wariness. Although they may be reluctant to socialize, giving in to this attitude will encourage rather than alleviate social stress.

Immaturity

Your adolescent Dachshund may be fully grown and look like an adult, but this does not guarantee the dog is capable of adult levels of behavior. Only time and maturity can improve a puppy's stamina, attention span, social skills, and confidence. Don't be tempted to expect too much too soon. During adolescence, training will be complicated by occasional transitions from puppy to adult behavior.

Stopping Trouble Before It Starts

Train proactively to prevent problems and revise them before they turn into entrenched habits. Every time an unwanted behavior is rewarded, it is more likely to be repeated. Almost every behavior is preceded by signals of intention. A good trainer perceives the dog's intentions and interrupts unwanted behavior before it reaches its inevitable conclusion. This may be enough to prevent habit formation without resorting to major corrective measures.

Discourage Nipping and Rough Play

You can inadvertently reinforce many bad habits simply by ignoring unwanted behavior. Never assume that jumping, barking, or nipping are temporary behaviors a puppy will outgrow. Although these behaviors usually become identified as

> **Training Tip**
> *Behavior problems can have a physical basis. Compulsive habits like persistent licking and scratching may be due to allergies or exposure to toxins.*
>
> *Obsessive attention-seeking behavior can be a symptom of Cushing's disease, hypothyroidism, cognitive dysfunction, or visual or auditory impairment.*
>
> *Sudden onset aggression can be due to pain from periodontal disease, arthritis, a urinary tract infection, or an endocrine imbalance such as hyperthyroidism. There is some evidence of a link between generalized anxiety and hypothyroidism. Some forms of cardiac disease can also produce physical symptoms similar to anxiety*
>
> *Chronic physical pain or Addison's Disease can also lead to generalized anxiety and personality changes.*

problems during adolescence they start much earlier. Mouthing and play biting are normal forms of canine interaction and a puppy easily forms the habit of initiating play by nipping and jumping on people. Never allow your pup to grab or pull at your clothes. If rough physical play is encouraged it will escalate. If you are excited, your dog becomes excited and adrenaline levels continue to rise. Any type of rough play, loud vocal corrections, or physical punishment will serve to intensify the response of a dog that is already in an aroused state of mind.

Daily interactive play is the only way to discourage nipping, so set boundaries to prevent rough play. React consistently

Training Tip

Dachshunds are masters at snatching contraband on the street. It's imperative to instill reliable commands for "drop it" and "leave it" to prevent your dog from ingesting potentially dangerous items.

Leave It

With your dog on a leash, walk towards an appealing item you have placed on the floor. As your dog reaches for it give a command to leave it, tell the dog to look at you, and reward the dog with an even more appealing treat. This can also be reinforced with a click as soon as the dog reorients to you. As your Dachshund gets the idea, begin

Most Dachshunds have trouble ignoring temptations like this. It may require some effort to teach them commands like "leave it" and "drop it."

using higher value items as a lure or placing them in accessible places such as on a low table. Don't try this exercise without the leash until your dog's response is very reliable. Otherwise, it will be nearly impossible to prevent a Dachshund from grabbing the illegal item. Some Dachshunds have real trouble with this concept. In that case, targeting may help reinforce the response to ignore temptation.

Drop It

It is easier to teach a puppy to relinquish something on command but dogs of every age can and should learn this response. The key is to reward voluntary cooperation rather than turning it into a confrontation. That is guaranteed to put the dog on the defensive.

Tug-of-war can be an easy method to teach your Dachshund to defer to you as pack leader and relinquish something on command. Initiate a tug game but stop tugging after a few seconds and simply hold your end of the toy. Give the drop it command, followed by the look command, make eye contact with the dog, and offer a food reward in exchange for the tug toy. Cooperation should always be praised and rewarded. Alternately, put your hand on a toy the dog is holding and offer a different item or a treat in its place. Practice these exercises frequently in situations you can control. Never chase the dog to enforce the command, or use verbal or physical punishment to get something away from the dog. This is more likely to reinforce the dog's instinct to guard the item, and you can be accidentally bitten.

whenever your pup's teeth touch your skin or playing becomes too rough. Stop playing and give a vocal warning.

Discourage Resource Guarding and Possessivness

The food dish is often a focal point of guarding behavior. Using aggressive displays to keep you at a distance is a learned habit that can evolve into an ongoing strategy to control resources. Your Dachshund should always willingly defer to human members of the household. Reinforcing this idea should never involve a confrontation. Reward cooperation and encourage trust. Make a habit of hanging around during your dog's mealtime, petting the dog, and touching the dish. Occasionally, take a few pieces of kibble from the dish and hand feed them to the dog. Teaching your dog to accept this is far easier than revising protective aggression later on. This is especially important if you have children who may wander near the dog during mealtime. This is a very common situation for dog bites to occur.

Discourage Attention-seeking Behavior

Attention-seeking behaviors like barking, whining, pawing, jumping, nipping, or following you around the house can be extremely annoying and difficult to revise. Although these are initiated by the dog, many owners unintentionally encourage them. Responding to the dog often ramps up the behavior by reinforcing underlying anxiety. Likewise, many dogs perceive a negative response as a rewarding form of attention. Many dogs resort to these behaviors in an effort to understand their environment, gain control, or assert social status. Although it may appear completely the opposite, attention seeking can be due to insecurity and stress from an unstable daily routine, inconsistent messages regarding rules, confused expectations, or simply a lack of attention.

Teach Stress Management and Impulse Control

Ensure that your Dachshund has sufficient daily mental and physical stimulation. Exercise needs vary, and some Dachshunds require quite a bit in order to unwind. If your Dachshund is not tired after a walk or play session, more exercise must be incorporated into the daily routine.

Dachshunds also need opportunities to investigate their environment. The urge

---

Tips to Discourage Attention-seeking Behavior

- *Refuse to respond to it in either positive or negative fashion.*
- *Reinforce a structured daily routine.*
- *Reduce stress factors such as boredom or excess energy that may contribute to it.*
- *Redirect the dog to a substitute activity like going for a walk when the first indications of compulsive behavior start.*

to sniff and explore is inherent in the breed and the mental stimulation it provides is just as important as physical activity for many dogs. Rather than trying to discourage this instinct, try using five-minute investigative breaks as a training reward. Simply knowing that this reward is coming can have a calming effect on the dog. If your Dachshund is experiencing significant problems with focus and attention, make your training sessions shorter and provide frequent breaks to play and sniff. Use a special command to tell your Dachshund when it is okay to take a break and watch closely. As soon as you see the dog reorienting to you, reinforce that response with a treat or click and get back to work.

Reinforcing Socialization and Training

The benefits of training and socialization will diminish unless they are reinforced from the close of a puppy's socialization period (12–14 weeks) until adulthood (12–18 months). Even well-socialized puppies may regress if socialization is subsequently neglected. Dachshunds are naturally prone to conflicting internal and external motivations that may undermine training or encourage wariness.

New habits are assimilated in three phases: learning the information, storing it as a memory, and developing the ability to access it when needed. The relative speed of this complex process is largely dependant on the survival value of the informa-

Teaching Your Dachshund to Shift Out of Prey Mode

Initiating and ending play sessions is an excellent way to instill impulse control but this may not be enough for dogs with strong prey drive. If your Dachshund needs extra work in this area use a special settle down command to reinforce it.

When your dog is calm initiate a tug of war game for five minutes. Before dog gets into total play frenzy give the look command, followed by a command to settle down. Praise and reward any effort to comply, even though this may be just a few seconds at first. Resume the game and repeat this exercise two or three times. Some Dachshunds may need daily practice for several weeks to instill an on off switch. Never give the dog an opportunity to completely run off the rails and lose control before giving the settle command. Practicing this exercise also helps you become aware of your dog's excitability threshold and how your behavior may contribute to it.

tion. Dogs learn many things after a single experience—recognizing dangers and food sources, for instance. Complex learned behaviors are generally less relevant to survival and thus more difficult to retain in long-term memory. There is also a strong genetic component to the reinforcement process based on a breed's sensory patterns. Dogs are designed to most efficiently retain olfactory memories and those connected with social acceptance but that varies according to individual and breed-specific sensory abilities and emotional

Short breaks to investigate the environment may improve your Dachshund's attention span during training.

thresholds. For instance, some breeds are naturally more attuned to social rewards. Dachshunds are more attuned to environmental payoffs.

- Consistently introduce your Dachshund to new people, places and things, even if you get a reluctant response.
- Vary your dog's routine such as changing the route of your daily walk or visiting an unfamiliar park.
- Enroll your Dachshund in a structured activity such as a daycare program or a training class.

Training Plateaus

Anyone who has tried his or her hand at Dachshund training is familiar with the breed's famous selective deafness. This is just one of the reactions responsible for their reputation for stubbornness and indifference. Dachshunds will resort to escape behavior if training leaves them bored, confused, or frustrated.

Competing motivations play a role in every training response. A strong motivation to perform a particular activity is always accompanied by the suppression of other desires. If the suppressed behavior happens to be a strong component of a dog's personality, it may eventually override the training and create a behavioral impasse of frustration and anxiety.

Frustration functions to divert attention and compel exploration for a more satisfying response. Dogs often resort to displacement activities such as constantly sniffing the ground, scratching an ear, or lip licking to diffuse pent up frustration and resolve conflicting reactions. It may also lead to unlearning an unrewarding behavior. It is not that unusual for a Dachshund to become progressively more uncooperative despite a handler's valiant attempts to encourage and motivate the dog's interest in training. This is usually due to boredom caused by too much regimented training. It is also possible that the dog is interpreting the handler's effort as a reward for apathetic behavior. In that case, you may want to experiment with a combination of correction and reinforcement to revive the dog's motivation.

Use Rewards Properly

Success is contingent on using the right reward at the right time. It must have genuine value for the dog, and it must be doled out purposefully to reinforce the connection to good performance. Varying rewards helps to prevent the dog from becoming fixated on environmental cues for them, but food, a clicker, or praise don't work equally well in every situation. The reward should be based on the behavior you want to encourage.

It's also essential to build a mystique around the reward. It must be something special, with limited availability. This conditions the dog to respond with maximum enthusiasm. If a reward is overly accessible, it loses its appeal. It is possible to make a particular reward seem more desirable by restricting access to the item, thus turning it into something special.

Vary the Routine

Training Dachshunds requires a good amount of patience and persistence. However, you must recognize when it's time to revise the routine or give the dog a break. Young or old, Dachshunds don't respond well to rigid, repetitive, lengthy training sessions. Scheduling frequent breaks for play or investigating the environment can help a young dog maintain enthusiasm for training and may also help an older dog cultivate a positive attitude about it.

Diversifying your training program can also help to maintain enthusiasm and promote a balanced temperament. Alternate training with a sport that your Dachshund enjoys like earth dog or tracking. This not only provides an outlet for prey drive, it also teaches the dog to shift mental skills to focus between various activities. This may initially result in slower progress, but it accomplishes something that is far more valuable. These types of activities will create an enduring rapport between dog and trainer.

A creative approach is essential to keeping your Dachshund motivated for training, especially if you have expectations of advanced training for competition. Top performance is dependent on a positive attitude and keeping it fun is critical to success.

When Training Hits a Wall

If training has come to a standstill, you'll need to reassess your methods and work hard to get things back on track.

9 *Remedial Training*

The Right Approach

Bad habits are not written in stone. Regardless of the cause, Dachshund reform is possible if you possess the time, patience, and willingness to implement a behavior modification program. Everyone in the household must take an active role in this effort to uniformly reinforce retraining. If you are seeking major changes in your Dachshund's behavior, break the process down to simple steps. Start small and give the dog opportunities to succeed at each stage. This gives you both a chance to develop confidence and a sense of achievement. Training takes time, and you will be disappointed if you are hoping for instant results. Expect three to four weeks of daily work to change a habit. In some cases, a lifetime of follow-up reinforcement may be needed.

Bad habits evolve for many reasons. Successfully revising them requires the right approach. You must identify the underlying factors responsible for motivating the behavior and understand your dog to determine how best to approach retraining.

Dachshunds possess a wide range of temperament traits; therefore, tailored behavior modification is essential. The last thing you want to do is inadvertently discourage good behavior in the process of revising bad habits. Your dog's temperament and response, not the rhetoric of any particular trainer, should be your ultimate guide. Lavishing food and praise to shape and reinforce new habits, while ignoring undesirable behavior, works well for some dogs. For others, a combination of praise and correction yields better results.

The Evolution of Habits

Habits are the product of learned associations between particular actions and consequences. These can be positive or negative, intended or accidental. The first step in revising them is to identify and remove the reinforcements. Dachshunds are extremely attuned to their environment and it's easy to miss subtle reinforcements or fail to recognize them for what they are.

For instance, if your Dachshund is addicted to attention-seeking behavior, a negative response from you still provides a form of reward, so it becomes equally important to avoid any response in that situation. Habits based in anxiety can become more entrenched in response to a reprimand. It is also normal for habits to initially escalate due to frustration once their pay off ceases, thus giving the impression that the retraining has failed.

Different Habits, Different Solutions

With practice, it becomes easier to categorize the various cause and effect reasons for particular behaviors. This provides a great deal of insight into the source and solution for specific problems. Start by analyzing the situation from a Dachshund perspective.

- Is this habit an expression of an instinctive drive?
- Is the habit an attempt to satisfy a basic need like physical exercise or social interaction?
- Is the habit a response to circumstances in the dog's life such as an unstructured routine with large periods of unsupervised time?
- Is the habit a result of your actions? For example, are you in the habit of getting your dog wound up when you arrive home?
- When did the behavior start? Puppyhood, adolescence, or a major change in the dog's routine may contribute to behavior patterns.
- How often does the behavior occur? Has it become more frequent?
- What factors trigger or intensify it? Does it occur in the presence of particular family members or other pets?
- Is the dog receiving consistent messages regarding household rules? You or other

family members may alternately encourage and reprimand the same behavior.
- Is the behavior limited to certain aspects of the daily routine or a specific location? For instance, possessiveness regarding food or territory often occurs in the kitchen during mealtime.

Identifying the common denominators gives you insights into the motivation and reward pattern that created the habit. That is your winning ticket to devise an effective reform strategy.

The first step in revising the problem is to make some changes in the dog's environment to prevent the behavior from occurring. A dog-proof trash container will prevent dumpster diving, but if your Dachshund is stealing trash to get attention or alleviate boredom, there's a bigger issue to address. A lasting solution requires both removing the temptation and changing the dog's routine to alleviate boredom.

From a survival standpoint, both avoidance and reward are equally powerful motivations to learn or revise a habit. Consistent punishment or physically preventing an undesirable behavior will cause the dog to suppress it, at least when you are around. The boredom, frustration, or anxiety that was originally responsible for causing the behavior will remain and eventually trigger the search for a new coping strategy. This is why negatively reinforced patterns inevitably become destabilized. This is true of random habits and systematic training. Classically conditioned learning is stronger than operant conditioning but any learned behavior will decline unless it is built on a good training foundation. In the case of Dachshunds, ineffective, inappropriate, or incomplete training can and does

Dachshunds constantly assess their environment for new information and change their behavior accordingly.

fall apart as soon as a more appealing motivation presents itself.

Tried-and-True Methods to Revise Bad Habits

Counter-conditioning revises the learned association responsible for a habit. A new incompatible behavior is encouraged and rewarded every time the dog engages in the unwanted habit. Rather than erasing the learned association, it is replaced by something you both perceive as more desirable.

Desensitization

Desensitization inhibits unwanted behavior by systematically raising a dog's response threshold to the contributing factors. Through repeated practice the dog learns to ignore triggers, distractions, and temptations responsible for the bad habit.

Systematically introduce the dog to these triggers, at levels that can be tolerated and ignored. Provide a satisfying alternative such as targeting, food rewards, or the *relax* command to redirect the dog's attention. As your Dachshund's ability to ignore distractions and maintain focus improves this alternative will replace the reward originally derived from the instinctive response.

Gradually introduce more challenges as your Dachshund's tolerance level increases. Proceed slowly and constantly monitor your dog's reactions. Your goal is to keep the dog below the threshold of arousal at all times.

Barking

Excessive barking ranks high on the list of Dachshund behavior issues. This doesn't imply that every noisy wiener dog is in the grip of a predetermined genetic directive. Nor is maladaptive barking something you must tolerate simply because you chose this breed.

In many cases, it is fueled by a mixture of motivations. Dachshund temperament can range from excitable and outgoing to suspicious and insecure. It is easy to misread the signals attached to these extremes as well as the huge spectrum of nuanced personalities in between. All Dachshunds are focused on their environment, but their responses towards it vary tremendously. In an outgoing dog, a keen interest in the environment might lead to excessive barking prompted by excitability. A naturally apprehensive Dachshund, equally focused on the surroundings, may think that a good offense is the best defense, and anxiety leads to chronic barking.

Either way, effective reform requires simultaneously discouraging the habit and treating the underlying motivation. Anti-bark collars may suppress the habit, but if the barking is due to anxiety, boredom, stress, or frustration it will find another outlet. If overexcitement is the underlying cause, reprimands will likely intensify the

dog's adrenaline level. A lasting solution involves redirecting the dog's response through counter-conditioning or desensitization to reduce the anxiety prompting the behavior.

Common Reasons for Barking

Boredom
Recreational barking is a means of alleviating boredom. Some dogs will get into this habit merely to keep themselves entertained. The habit is most common in dogs left alone for long periods. The resultant barking becomes compulsive and self-rewarding. Limit unsupervised access to situations that trigger barking such as looking out of the window or spending time alone outdoors. Provide more structure to the dog's routine and use counter-conditioning to interrupt the pattern and instill a new response.

Attention-Seeking
Demanding barking continually escalates as it is reinforced either unconsciously or in an attempt to quiet the dog. The dog is rewarded with control of the environment and the agenda. All family members must

> **Training Tip**
> *Tug-of-war can be used to reduce the anxiety that triggers barking. Engaging in play shifts your dog from defensive to prey drive, promotes calmness and confidence, and serves as a good distraction. It is also impossible for the dog to bark while holding a toy.*

stop rewarding the behavior. Control the dog's access to valuable items like food and toys and adhere to a daily routine. Counter-condition a new response such as giving the command *sit* whenever the dog commences barking. Teaching the dog to retrieve or carry a toy can also work as a replacement behavior. It gives the dog something to do and makes it impossible to bark.

Self-Protection

Defensive barking is meant keep potentially dangerous individuals at a distance. Fueled by anxiety, it becomes self-perpetuating. Banishing your dog to a crate, backyard, or another room to stop the barking often intensifies the existing anxiety.

Use the *relax* command to systematically reward calmness in situations that normally provoke barking. Use desensitization exercises to reduce the dog's anxiety levels in specific situations.

Warning of Intruders

Territorial barking is an instinctive response exhibited by all dogs, but five or six barks is plenty. Dachshunds that are highly reactive or overly fixated on their environment may overreact to potential threats. The resulting inability to distinguish between significant and minor details of the environment can lead to chronic anxiety and nonstop barking.

Use a house leash to interrupt the barking sequence as soon as it commences. Counter-condition an alternate response such as the *relax* command. Systematically desensitize the dog to environmental triggers.

Under no circumstances attempt to discipline the dog by shouting "Shut up!" or

> **Training Tip: Play Games**
> *Most dogs retain a lifetime interest in chewing but normally become more discriminating about it as they mature. You can encourage this by turning it into a game of "Find the Chew Toy," which also reinforces the drop it and leave it commands.*
>
> *Place a mixture of toys and contraband items on the floor and allow your Dachshund to check them out. Use a clicker or food treats to reward every sign of interest in appropriate items. Give the drop it or leave it command whenever the dog gravitates to your shoe, glove or TV remote. Your Dachshund will learn this concept faster than you think, dogs possess an excellent ability to discriminate between individual items.*

"Be quiet." The dog is already anxious and aroused, and loud reprimands will only intensify that reaction.

Destructive Chewing

Dogs constantly use their mouths to investigate their environment. Puppies may do this more obsessively but don't assume this is something your Dachshund will outgrow. Chewing is self-rewarding. It alleviates boredom, releases endorphins, and eases stress.

Chewing can turn into an obsession due to stress or boredom. In those situations you must treat the underlying problem as well as the outward behavior. Uncontrolled chewing can be a real safety

Use games like "find the chew toy" to help your puppy recognize the difference between chew toys and new shoes.

hazard, leading to intestinal blockage, poisoning, or injuries.

- Dog-proof with a vengeance until you get this problem under control.
- Provide several safe, interesting chew toys. Rotating these toys may help maintain the dog's interest in them.
- Supervise carefully to redirect chewing away from inappropriate items. A house leash may be helpful for this.
- If your Dachshund has a special fondness for chewing specific items, applications of Vick's or Bitter Apple may discourage the desire.

Nipping

Puppies learn bite control from their dam, and this concept is later reinforced as they play with other dogs. Unless they are deprived of opportunities to interact with their dam and littermates, puppies learn to control their jaw power by 18 weeks of age. A playmate may respond aggressively or refuse to continue playing after a painful nip. If a pup accidentally inflicts pain when playing with a littermate, the reaction is a loud yelp and the puppy learns to bite gently during play. However, this idea must be regularly reinforced until adulthood.

Puppies often become overexcited and inadvertently nip when playing with humans. Some also get into the habit of mouthing an owner's hand as a playful gesture or sign of affection. Eventually this behavior can be used for opportunistic rank enhancement or attention seeking. During play, dogs regularly use their mouth and teeth in attempts to revise the hierarchy of the relationships with dogs *and* humans.

Although it begins early, biting usually does not become an issue until adolescence, when a pup's strength and jaw power increase. Nor is it unusual for a Dachshund to flip into prey mode and lose control during wild play. Play mode is actually prey mode and a prey bite can do considerable damage.

As pack leader you should always initiate play and set boundaries to prevent your dog from losing control. If your Dachshund mouths, nips, or growls during play, respond immediately. Look into the dog's eyes and assertively respond with a *no* followed by a time out. Regardless of whether it is accidental or intentional, all family members must consistently reinforce the same response to nipping.

It's easy to become annoyed when your Dachshund nips but your reaction to this misbehavior must be calm and calculated. Responding in an agitated or confrontational manner can make things worse by encouraging the dog to become defensive or aggressive.

Food Guarding

The survival instinct to compete for food represents a puppy's first introduction to pack mentality. This competitive motivation can lead to food guarding in pups as young as eight weeks. It is definitely not something a puppy will outgrow and usually becomes a noticeable problem between 6–18 months, motivated by opportunistic dominance or anxiety.

Possessiveness or hostility during mealtime includes growling, snapping, or baring teeth when a person or another pet approaches the food dish. Unchecked, it can escalates into aggression in other situations.

Until the problem is under control, manage the dog's environment to minimize incidents. These steps are especially important if you have children or multiple pets.

- Feed the dog in a crate.
- Do not free feed.
- Remove access to toys or chews that trigger guarding.
- Restrict access to rooms or situations that provoke guarding such as allowing the dog to beg at the dinner table.

Use desensitization to build the dog's tolerance level for these sitations. Consistently reward non-aggressive behavior

Dumpster Diving

Foraging is a normal part of the prey behavior sequence and if your Dachshund manages to accomplish one successful garbage raid it can be sufficient to create a habit that is both annoying and dangerous.

Reprimanding the dog will likely produce one reliable alteration in the behavior pattern: the sneaky garbage raid. Your pet will simply wait until the coast is clear to resume his search for treasure in the trash. For your dog's safety, keep trashcans out of reach or invest in a dog-proof container. Teach your Dachshund the "drop it" and "leave it" commands to prevent ingesting dangerous items.

This is not the way to discourage your pup from begging at the table.

with praise and high value treats like cheese or liverwurst that are more enticing than the food in the dog's dish. Sit near the dish while your dog eats and employ the following exercises.

- Periodically touch the dog during meal-time.
- Hand feed a few pieces of food.
- Pick up the dish and replace it while the dog is eating.

If the dog begins to behave posses-sively in response to your presence near the food bowl, take it down a notch. If necessary, give the dog a fifteen-minute time out to calm down.

Ongoing behavior modification may be necessary to keep this problem in check.

Do not attempt this behavior modifica-tion exercise if you feel it is too risky. Con-sult a qualified behaviorist.

Begging

Barking, whining, jumping, pawing, drool-ing, and staring are guaranteed to disrupt your dinnertime. That is not the only draw-back. Begging at the table can also result in your dog ingesting poisonous or dangerous pilfered items; it is also a major contributor to Dachshund obesity. Bad from many angles, this is one habit you must take credit for. Puppies instinctively beg for food during weaning but adult dogs quickly teach them to keep this behavior in check. Once a puppy goes to a new home, begging is effortlessly reinforced via operant condition-ing. Only one family member needs to encourage it to ensure the dog becomes a relentless beggar. Unless you are prepared to live with this, do not encourage it.

If it's too late for that, take heart. Unlike some bad habits, this one is fairly easy to stop if everyone cooperates with the retraining process. Your Dachshund should be fed, exercised, and crated before you sit down to dinner. Provide a chew toy to keep the dog occupied in the crate. If demand barking ensues, all members of the household must be prepared to ignore it. Begging and complaining will probably increase before ceasing. Your resourceful Dachshund may also experiment with new strategies to get food or attention.

Picky Eating

Any dog can be turned into a fussy eater if the owner puts enough time and effort into the job. Dogs immediately understand when they are being rewarded for finicky eating habits. After causing the problem

Dogs are creatures of habit. A consistent mealtime routine is the key to good eating habits.

■ Provide no between-meal snacks.
■ Always serve the food in a clean dish
■ Use the same type of dish (flat, deep, ceramic, stainless steel, etc.). consistently; many dogs will not eat from an unfamiliar dish.
■ Avoid changing foods, as your Dachshund may be reluctant to try something unfamiliar. If you must change brands or types, do so gradually, mixing the old food with the new.
■ Warm the food to make it more appealing.
■ Most dogs prefer textured, rather than very wet or mushy food.
■ Sprinkle a tablespoon of flavorful topping over the food. Tuna, lean chicken or hamburger, shredded cheese, and crumbled bacon are all effective appetite stimulants.

many owners make matters worse in their attempts to resolve it. Catering to fussy eating habits not only intensifies the problem, it can encourage related opportunistic dominance behaviors.

If a thorough veterinarian check reveals no physical basis for a chronically poor appetite, the reason is psychological. Revising poor eating habits through behavior modification may take three or four weeks. To combat the problem

■ Offer only the dog's customary food.
■ Remove the dish after 20 minutes even if the dog has eaten only a little. (Dry food can be offered again at the next regular meal but wet food should be discarded.)

Digging

Dachshunds are mentally and physically designed to dig, making this self-rewarding habit tough to revise. It's instinctive and can be intensified by a need to relieve anxiety. Digging is also self-perpetuating: as the dog resorts to it more often, it becomes addicting.

Digging not only wrecks your flowerbeds and leaves your Dachshund filthy, it can also lead to escapes. Some dogs transfer the habit indoors, digging through mattresses, carpets, and couch cushions. Identify possible contributing factors such as boredom, stress, weather-related discomfort, or environmental triggers.

■ Is your Dachshund seeking a safe retreat due to fear or anxiety?

99

- Does your Dachshund need more mental or physical activity?
- Does your Dachshund have adequate protection from sun and heat outdoors?
- Are there burrowing rodents in your yard encouraging your Dachshund's predatory instinct?
- Does your Dachshund customarily bury chew toys or bones?

The desire to dig cannot be prevented but you can control it through a combination of supervision, management, and counterconditioning. Some breeders also recommend setting aside a special area in the garden where the dog is permitted to dig.

Dachshunds are built to squeeze through tight spaces. Never underestimate their ability to tunnel and escape.

Escape Artists

Escaping and roaming can be triggered by predatory drive. The sight of a squirrel or scent of a mouse can activate your Dachshund's predatory sequence including a determined desire to dig or chase. It is also self-reinforcing. Once a dog does it, it's more likely to happen again. Don't let your Dachshund develop a taste for running away.

1. Reinforce fencing with underground barriers or brickwork along fence perimeters to prevent tunneling.
2. Don't allow your Dachshund to run away from you in a large fenced yard. Keep the dog contained in a smaller area or use a long check cord to maintain some control until you have established a strong bond.
3. Never stop practicing a recall command, no matter how well trained your Dachshund may be.
4. Frequently practice the *look* command when you are outdoors to reinforce your Dachshund's ability to focus and ignore distractions. A clicker is helpful to instantly reward your dog for staying within close range.
5. Use counter-conditioning to revise chasing or digging habits that lead to consequent escape attempts. When you notice your Dachshund revving up to chase something, interrupt before the dog loses focus and provide a more rewarding alternative.
6. Neutering may help curb this problem in males but will be more effective if combined with other retraining and behavior modification techniques.

Housetraining Lapses

Lapses in housetraining can be due to mental, physical, or environmental reasons. Begin by ruling out possible physical causes such as a sudden dietary change, revised feeding schedule, or side effect of a new medication. A thorough veterinarian exam will detect any illness that may be the underlying cause.

If this does not provide a solution, examine the dog's routine. The problem may be due to a recent change in the dog's exercise schedule or territory, such as losing access to a preferred elimination spot. Fear and anxiety can also inhibit a dog from

Plenty of patience, positive reinforcement, and a consistent schedule can reform the housetraining delinquent.

Retraining Tips

To ensure predictable compliance for any behavior revision start small, build on reliable skills, gradually add distractions and variables, and never give the dog a chance to backslide. If your Dachshund has two housetraining lapses in a row, go back to square one reinforcing the routine.

- *Keep track of when and where accidents happen. If you cannot figure this out, better supervision is definitely in order. Extra walks or revisions to the feeding schedule may solve the problem if accidents occur predictably. You may need to tinker with your dog's schedule but major alterations are more likely to exacerbate the problem.*
- *Thoroughly clean all traces of past accidents and curtail access to parts of the house where they regularly happen. Crate or supervise your dog at all times indoors.*
- *Implement a standard elimination schedule with particular emphasis on reward and reinforcement.*

eliminating in a customary spot. This can stem from possibilities as diverse as fears of street noise, a neighbor's aggressive dog, or negative reinforcement, creating a reluctance to eliminate in your presence.

If your Dachshund customarily goes out alone to eliminate, supervise to see what's actually going on. Some Dachshunds are notoriously reluctant to go out and do their business in bad weather despite their hardy heritage.

When you send your dog outside to eliminate, make sure that's what really happens.

You may need to reexamine your expectations. You may be expecting too much from a young puppy or assuming that your dog is completely housetrained when the job was only half done.

When introducing an adult Dachshund into your household, it is advisable to spend a few weeks reinforcing housetraining procedures, whether or not this seems necessary. This becomes even more important when working with a rescue dog. Supervision should be ongoing for six months to a year.

Involuntary Urination

Excitement or anxiety can trigger involuntary urination. Triggers can vary from happy expectation to fearful submission in a variety of circumstances. This problem is most common in puppies, especially those neutered at a very young age. It is usually confined to specific situations and many cases resolve with maturity. However, human factors can intensify or reinforce the problem. Regardless of the cause, the more often it happens the more likely it is to happen again.

Ignore accidents and concentrate on behavior modification. Gradually condition the dog to remain calm and relaxed enough to maintain bladder control. This may involve desensitizing a nervous dog or counter-conditioning an excitable dog. This particular problem is a dog/owner collaboration and revising it requires the same.

Know your dog. If your Dachshund goes over the top when you arrive home, a loud or emotional response will discourage self-control. Likewise, if your Dachshund is inherently apprehensive, resist the urge to offer any type of greeting. Saying *hello*, reaching down, or making eye contact can cause a fearful dog to lose bladder control.

For an excitable dog, instill a competing behavior such as sitting on command when you arrive home. For a nervous dog, keep your greeting low key and begin your interaction with the *relax* command about ten minutes after you get home.

In either case, basic obedience training may help boost a dog's self-control and confidence in order to overcome extreme emotional reactions.

Territorial Marking

Housetraining can fall apart during adolescence due to social stress or hormonal surges. Leg lifting may start at five or six months and become a persistent habit by 12 to 18 months. It is most common in intact males, but all dogs are instinctively programmed to mark their territory with urine because this is their preferred olfactory communication method. These messages disperse slowly through the environment and linger long after any encounter. This makes them ideal for communicating important canine information such as territorial boundaries, status, and personal details. It also explains why it is

so important to thoroughly clean up all traces of urine marking when trying to revise this habit.

Territorial urination increases a dog's confidence and security providing an ongoing motivation to saturate the territory. A dog may obsessively mark the same location and make a special target of anything new or unfamiliar in the environment.

Although it has social, territorial, and sexual connotations it has a sizeable learned component and will therefore respond to normal housetraining procedures.

Curbing this habit requires reinforcing basic rules but this can be tricky for Dachshunds. Territorial marking is preceded by a predictable sequence, but Dachshund leg lifting can be hard to spot. Supervision is critical. Verbal corrections to interrupt the leg-lifting sequence may also help. However, overdoing it will intensify any underlying anxiety. If you don't feel confident about your timing or approach, don't even try it.

■ Scrupulously clean up all areas the dog has targeted.
■ Prevent access to these locations until retraining is complete.
■ Implement the normal housetraining schedule.
■ Training pants or bellybands will prevent the dog from actually marking any territory and often inhibit the behavior.
■ Neutering can also be effective but if the habit has already formed it must be combined with retraining.

10 *Dachshunds with Special Needs*

Because Dachshunds are so popular it's inevitable that a few will suffer from unusual problems that complicate training. A behaviorist can offer solutions for many of these. In other cases, common sense and the advice of experienced owners offers the best remedy.

Be prepared to use plenty of encouragement and treats when training a senior Dachshund.

The Older Dachshund

Dogs of any age can learn new tricks, but older Dachshunds are not typically thrilled about change, especially when they involve alterations in their normal routine or environment. This can cause an easygoing dog to become nervous or confused, leading to anxiety or avoidance. An underlying physical basis such as cognitive dysfunction, chronic pain, or failing eyesight also factors in to behavior. When retraining an older Dachshund your approach must be tailored to the dog's temperament, tolerance levels, and physical abilities.

There are many reasons why senior Dachshunds are resistant to training. Some are generally laid back, rather unmotivated, and slow to respond. Engaging and maintaining their attention for training can be the biggest challenge. Use plenty of vocal encouragement and treats. Any type of correction can completely turn them off so be patient and keep training sessions short. Training should not become a source of anxiety, but for some dogs this is inevitable. This can lead to avoidance behavior as the dog seeks to escape the stressful situation. Getting past this obstacle requires a calm persistent approach. Running away or refusal to cooperate should not be tolerated. If this approach succeeds, the dog will make it a habit. Be calm and persistent. Try a slightly different approach if necessary, but don't take no for an answer.

Almost as many seniors fall into the category of stubborn and aloof. They don't want to pay attention; they may simply ignore you or escape the scene when the subject of training comes up. You need to be persistent and ensure the dog takes you seriously but don't be tempted to turn it into a showdown. That is guaranteed to reinforce the problems you're already dealing with.

Extinction

Retraining to discourage ingrained habits may require ongoing counter-conditioning to keep things heading in the right direction. Abandoning habits that are no longer rewarding is known as extinction. This process does not erase the memory of a learned habit. Once that gem has been filed away in your Dachshund's brain it's there to stay. Rather than disappearing, it is replaced by something perceived as more relevant. However, this new response is always vulnerable to the interference from those lurking memories.

Successful retraining requires removing reinforcements that cause the unwanted behavior and making an alternate option more appealing. Together, these steps create a preference for a new behavior. If the old habit happens to be an instinctive pattern, this may require steady reinforcement to maintain the new response.

Remedial Socialization

It's not unusual for an adult Dachshund to be apprehensive when first entering a new home and some require extensive acclimation time or remedial socialization. If possible, have some items on hand from the dog's former home such as used bedding with a familiar scent. If you have information about the dog's previous daily routine adhere to it as much as possible to ease the transition. It is especially important to implement a housetraining routine regardless of whether the dog is already trained.

If your Dachshund does not begin adjusting after three weeks, start with a vet check to rule out physical reasons, such as a metabolic or neurological disorder. If possible find out if there are contributing factors in the dog's history such as a lack of early socialization or traumatizing experiences. Don't jump to these conclusions without evidence. It is easy to assume that a dog's fearfulness is due to previous mistreatment, but this won't help solve the problem if your guess is incorrect.

Rescue Dachshunds

Because this breed is so popular, unwanted Dachshunds have become an unhappy reality. Adopting a rescue dog is emotionally rewarding, but good intentions don't automatically ensure a good outcome. If you decide to take in a rescue dog, be prepared to provide a permanent home. Never take on this responsibility if you cannot make that promise.

Senior dogs can and do learn new tricks, although they may not exhibit boundless enthusiasm for the project.

Planning the adoption process gives you an idea what you are getting into and makes the transition far easier. Many shelters and rescue groups temperament test dogs prior to placement in order to gauge personality traits like stability, shyness, confidence, protectiveness, prey drive, and defensiveness. This process helps to ensure a better match. For instance, a Dachshund with high prey drive won't be put into a home with cats or other small pets. Temperament evaluation also helps predict a dog's ability to adapt to a new environment and respond to training, but it is far from foolproof.

■ Many shelter dogs have never been properly trained or socialized. Existing behavior problems are likely to be magnified in a shelter environment.

Dachshunds coming from commercial situations with no previous socialization or training, may easily adapt to the kennel-type atmosphere of a shelter, but may subsequently have trouble adjusting to the constant attention, social stress, and sudden introduction of rules in a typical home. The resulting confusion can trigger aggression, home destruction, or separation anxiety.

■ Temperament test results may vary substantially if the dog is retested after having time to adjust to that environment or having the opportunity to adjust to one less stressful such as a foster home. Results are also likely to be more accurate if the dog is removed from a distracting environment. Underlying medical conditions affecting behavior should also be taken into account when evaluating test results. These are often undiagnosed in shelter situations.

■ Many Dachshunds are naturally reserved and temperament tests focus specifically on traits that may not be their strong points, such as willingness to approach and accept strangers, tolerance for handling, or quick response to commands.

Adopting your Dachshund from a rescue group rather than a shelter has advantages. Rescue Dachshunds are generally placed in temporary foster care, where they receive remedial socialization and training before placement. Living with the dog in a typical home situation also provides opportunities to gain more realistic insights into the dog's temperament and potential adjustment problems.

Rescue groups take pains to evaluate their dogs in order to accurately match them to new homes. They also provide ongoing support for new owners after placement.

Temperament extremes exhibited by some rescue Dachshunds can complicate training. Once you recognize the problem you are dealing with, you can select the right training tools to manage them

Some rescue Dachshunds are prone to hyperactivity. They are extremely exuberant, excitable, friendly, and constantly shifting into play mode. When training this type of dog don't overdo the praise. Be firm and consistent. Quick accurate timing of rewards and corrections is essential. Clicker training may be perfect but you may need to install an on/off switch for playtime before any serious training is accomplished.

Many rescues are initially fearful and nervous. Provide plenty of adjustment time in a calm reassuring environment. During training avoid loud vocal tones, fast hand movements, and any type of vocal or leash correction. For some dogs it may be better to avoid any vocal interaction at first. Limit yourself to expressions and gestures. Keep training sessions short to minimize anxiety. Shaping can help build the dog's confidence and create interest in training.

Another common problem in rescue Dachshunds is extreme vigilance. These dogs obsessively focus on sights, sounds, and scents in their environment. They tend to be constantly distracted and easily stressed by motion or noise. The first step in training involves helping them learn to focus, ignore distractions, and improve their attention span. Targeting can be a

Daily interaction is the basis of a strong bond.

helpful technique to encourage focus and calmness by giving the dog some control over the environment. Short training sessions with many breaks to investigate and sniff can also be beneficial.

Even if your rescue Dachshund is stable and well adjusted, you must establish a rapport with the dog to facilitate effective communication. The amount of time needed to successfully bond with a rescue Dachshund depends on many factors, including age, life experience, and temperament. It may take just few days, or require months of patient effort, for the dog to settle into his new home. Don't plan on doing much productive training until it happens.

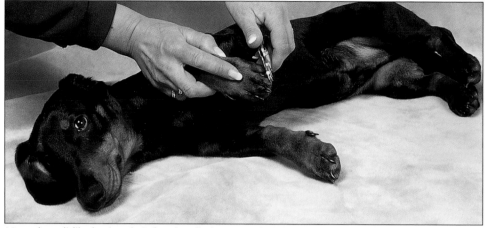

Many dogs dislike having their feet handled. Use gradual desensitization to help your dog overcome this fear.

Insecurity stemming from an unstable bond creates anxiety, resistance, and disinterest, making it impossible for the dog to focus and learn. A strong bond is the product of positive interactions within a consistent daily routine. Activities like going for walks, playing, and seeing to the dog's daily care continuously reinforce this message. Praise and treats can be used to shape desirable behaviors before you start formal training.

Behaviorists refer to rewards that dogs instinctively want, such as food, as *primary positive reinforcers*. Even a completely untrained Dachshund should respond to food. This doesn't automatically guarantee that a rescue dog will willingly take a treat from your hand—or do it politely. That is a learned behavior. Dogs suffering from behavior issues may require time, patience, and a great deal of encouragement to respond appropriately to typical rewards like hand feeding or petting.

Distrust of One Person in the Household

Occasionally an adult Dachshund bonds quickly to a new family but remains suspicious of one particular person. In some cases this can involve everyone else in the household. Typically, the dog avoids this person, rather than displaying outright fear. Forcing the dog to interact can escalate it into defensive aggression. Inciting a fear reaction will also serve to reinforce the behavior. There are ways to remedy the situation.

- ■ If possible this person should take over an important aspect of the dog's daily routine like feeding, grooming, or walking.
- ■ If the dog is reluctant to accept this, the person should always be present when these activities take place, thereby becoming associated with the experience.

- Occasionally, they should initiate brief, positive, low-key interactions like making eye contact, or praising or patting the dog. These encounters may seem inconsequential, but it does not work that way in the Dachshund think tank. Brief, subtle, positive encounters often work better than purposeful efforts to befriend a fearful dog.
- Give the dog a *relax* command when this person is in the room.
- Use targeting to encourage the dog to approach this person, or simply tolerate their presence. Since this is a voluntary action, the dog should feel more controlled and confident.

Fear of Handling or Grooming

A major roadblock to the bonding process is a reluctance to be touched or handled. This can be due to poor socialization, traumatic experiences, or inherent shyness. The end result can make vet exams, routine grooming, or normal interactions problematic.

Desensitization exercises should be done twice daily when the dog is calm and content, such as after dinner or a walk. Many dogs are especially reluctant to have their feet, faces, or hindquarters touched. Begin by handling parts of the dog least likely to trigger objections and move on to problem areas as the dog becomes more tolerant. Gradually extend the sessions from two minutes to ten minutes, employing more deliberate strokes as the dog's acceptance improves.

Don't attempt this exercise if you feel there is any risk of being bitten.

- Sit in a quiet comfortable spot with the dog next to you.
- Speak reassuringly while offering treats with one hand and using the other to touch the dog for one or two minutes.
- Constantly monitor the dog's reaction for fear or tension. Provide plenty of encouragement and reassurance.
- Stop the exercise at any sign of panic or aggression.
- Pushing the dog too fast will intensify the problem.

Physical Factors Complicating Training

Physical handicaps common in this breed include blindness, deafness, and back problems ranging from pain to paralysis. None of these troubles rule out the possibility of starting or continuing your relationship with the dog. Dachshunds are tough, adaptable, and resourceful. Unlike us, they rarely focus on their physical shortcomings. They live in the moment and instinctively try to make the best of any situation. Like all aspects of Dachshund training, think outside the box when working with a handicapped dog. Use sensible precautions but allow the dog enough freedom to figure out coping solutions.

Blindness and Deafness

Resist the urge to treat blind or deaf Dachshunds differently. You may want to coddle your dog but maintaining a regular routine is better for the dog in the long run. If given the opportunity they will demonstrate a surprising ability to compensate for their handicap using their other senses. For instance, blind Dachshunds rarely have trouble learning the layout of a house. They use their nose and whiskers to feel their way around like a cat. Many of them will navigate an unfamiliar room by walking alongside the walls to learn where doors, steps, and furniture are located. A deaf dog will learn a household routine based on visual rather than auditory clues.

Both deaf and blind dogs can be amazingly easy to housetrain because they pay close attention to details and rely so heavily on their sense of smell.

Both deaf and blind dogs can be extremely startled if approached or touched

unexpectedly, such as when they are sleeping. These frightening incidents can lead to a defensive response and this can turn into a habit if it happens frequently. Always provide a warning of your approach and give the dog time to wake up and become oriented before being touched or handled. This is especially important if you have children or other pets. If the dog gets into the habit of an instantaneous defensive response in certain situations, anyone wandering into them can be perceived as a threat.

Blind and deaf dogs are more likely to wander off and become lost. You may want to put a tag on your dog's collar noting the disability. If lost, they are at much greater risk of accidental injury from road traffic or attack from other dogs for obvious reasons.

It is also difficult to assess when a blind or deaf dog isn't feeling well. They don't always provide the subtle clues that owners normally rely on to make these determinations.

Helping Your Blind Dachshund
Although this is difficult to comprehend from a human standpoint, eyesight ranks fourth in importance as a canine sense. Blind dogs tend to be impressively resourceful, whether they are blind from birth or lose their sight later on. They instinctively compensate by relying on their olfactory, auditory, and tactile senses. Blind Dachshunds need opportunities to practice navigating their home territory and this will inevitably involve bumping into things. Dog-proof your home to prevent accidents in obvious danger spots like sharp corners on low furniture, staircases, swimming

Congenital deafness is more common in dogs with blue eyes, sometimes known as walleye, or large patches of white on their ears or head.

pools, and decks. It may be safest to keep some rooms off limits and restrict access with doorway gates. Always leave the dog's crate door open and never leave the dog unattended on a piece of furniture.

Help your blind Dachshund adjust by providing sensory clues to denote important aspects of the environment. For instance, different surfaces will help the dog recognize specific areas. Dogs discriminate easily between gravel, carpet, mulch, concrete, and linoleum. Distinctive sounds and scents also help the dog identify various locations. A bell on the kitchen door can help the dog navigate in and out.

Bells on collars can help a blind dog locate the whereabouts of other pets in the household and keep you informed of possible wandering.

Toys that make noise or have a scent will be easier for the dog to find.

For safety, a blind dog should be walked on a short lead, never a flex lead. Never permit unfamiliar people or dogs to approach or touch your blind dog unexpectedly during a walk.

A blind dog will orient to the sound of your voice, and this will become your primary training tool. Use plenty of distinct commands including cautions such as *stop* and *careful*, as well as directional cues like *left, right, back,* and *ahead.* Use the clicker, praise, and treats to reinforce behavior. Touch also becomes a much more important training tool.

During housetraining escort the dog on lead and provide plenty of reinforcements for a job well done. It also helps to use an easily recognizable surface such as mulch or gravel to designate the elimination area.

Blind Dachshunds should be fed in a crate to prevent food guarding. They are more likely to be protective about their food because they cannot see who is nearby.

Training Your Deaf Dachshund

Although dogs depend heavily on their sense of hearing, they rely more on vision to interpret your body language and understand cues during training. Deaf Dachshunds tend to be quite visually oriented and this can be used to a training advantage. When working with a deaf dog, always remain conscious of your body language, hand movements, and facial expressions to avoid sending the wrong message. Make frequent eye contact to ensure that the dog has opportunities to read your facial expressions.

Other than the fact that hand signals will be your primary communication method the process does not differ substantially from the methods you would use to train any dog.

All family members must use the same signals and some trainers use American Sign Language when communicating with deaf dogs. Start by teaching an attention signal, such as *look.* Deaf Dachshunds may be easily distracted by constant visual scanning. Work in a distraction-free environment with the dog on lead. You must also teach a hand signal that can be used to interrupt unwanted behavior, such as *sit,* and a recall command, since deaf dogs are more prone to wander off.

Many deaf dogs are also prone to excessive barking and a *quiet* or *settle* command will come in handy.

At first, it may require up to 50 repetitions for the dog to make the connection

Training Tip: Good Vibrations

A vibrating collar is similar to a vibrating phone or pager. The unit, attached to the dog's collar, is approximately the size of a bar of soap. A hand-held remote device is used to send signals to vibrate the collar.

The collar should fit snugly so the unit rests against the dog's skin. Give the dog two or three days to adjust to wearing it before activating it. Training the dog to orient to the vibration is similar to teaching a hearing dog to respond to a clicker. After about 20 repetitions the dog should associate the vibration with a treat. At that point, you can use it to get the dog's attention in order to give hand signals.

This collar will not help if you are working with a Dachshund that is reluctant to respond or pay attention for some other reason. That issue must be resolved first.

When using the vibrating collar, work closely with the dog, so you can use your hand to reinforce the pay attention response, if necessary. Add distractions very slowly.

This collar may also be helpful when working with an older dog that has become hearing impaired.

between the response and the gesture. Food treats can also be used for shaping behavior.

Some owners have better luck getting the dog's attention with a tactile cue such as a vibration. This can be accomplished by clapping your hands or stamping your foot, but more often, a vibrating collar is used.

Spinal Problems

Dachshunds unquestionably suffer from a higher than average incidence of herniated or ruptured disks due to thin brittle cartilage disks cushioning the vertebra. These problems are diagnosed most frequently in Dachshunds between four years and seven years of age, even though the underlying causative factors have been there all along.

The potential for back trouble cannot always be detected via physical exam or x rays. Environmental factors and poor physical condition certainly play a role, but it's also traceable to genetic predisposition. Back trouble is more prevalent in commercially bred puppies. Dedicated breeders work to eliminate the problem through selective breeding and some lines of Dachshunds are virtually free of back trouble.

Preventative Care

Breeders have differing philosophies regarding the dangers of allowing Dachshunds to jump or climb. Some feel these behaviors needlessly intensify the risk of back problems. Others believe that athleticism encourages strength and flexibility to help prevent back trouble. This remains open to debate. However, if your Dachshund has experienced one episode of disk disease, the odds of it happening again are substantial. These dogs must be watched carefully for any indication of relapse and supervised to prevent risky behavior. The most important preventative measure is ensuring the dog remains on all four legs, rather than two, to provide maximum back support at all times. Dachshunds are naturally hardy and many will continue to engage in rambunctious behavior despite the warning signs of pain. Retraining is often necessary to prevent a Dachshund from jumping, climbing, and roughhousing. All family members must cooperate to forbid the dog's attempts to climb or jump using a combination of consistent training and diligent supervision. *Relax* or *settle* can be used to reinforce calmness. Wearing a house leash for a couple of weeks can help your Dachshund get with the program as you teach and reinforce a *no jumping* command.

Gates or ramps in some parts of your home may also help prevent problems. Always lift or carry the dog in a horizontal position carefully supporting the back.

It's also imperative to keep the dog at a healthy weight.

Back pain should always be suspected if your Dachshund suddenly objects to being picked up or carried, or does not want to go outdoors or walk on the lead.

Whining and crying due to pain may be the first indication of a back problem but many owners don't put two and two together until the dog develops noticeable weakness causing a stumbling, staggering gait in the rear. At this stage, pain subsides, but paralysis may progress rapidly producing complete loss of movement, including bladder and bowel control.

In cases where surgery is not recommended treatment involves medical management and enforced rest. The dog must be confined to a crate or a very small pen for two to four weeks while receiving daily doses of vitamin supplements and anti-inflammatory medication. Strict rest is essential to promote healing and prevent additional damage to the spinal cord. You

If your dog has experienced an episode of spinal trouble, jumping should be consistently discouraged.

will be very grateful if you have trained your Dachshund to accept crating and handling. If not, be prepared for challenges that will require a combination of positive reinforcement, counter-conditioning, and plenty of patience.

Rehabilitation

After two to four weeks of enforced rest, your Dachshund will be able to resume

113

some level of activity in conjunction with ongoing physical therapy. These exercises may need to be done two or three times daily to improve mobility and prevent muscle atrophy. Be prepared to use plenty of food rewards, targeting, or clicker reinforcements to encourage cooperation with therapy sessions, because they must be done.

Swimming therapy can be done in a bathtub or wading pool. The water should be at chest level and the dog should be encouraged to calmly walk or paddle about in the water. Many dogs are apprehensive about this at first, but quickly begin to enjoy it.

Dachshunds are always anxious to walk as soon as they regain some strength. Use a body sling to support the dog's back, and encourage efforts to walk for a few

> ### Training Tip: Administering Pills
> *Some Dachshunds also object vigorously to taking pills. It may help to hide the pill in a treat that can be easily rolled into a tiny ball. You want your Dachshund to swallow it whole rather than dissecting it to discover the pill. Sooner or later most Dachshunds get wise to this trick. In that case, it is sometimes possible to trick the dog into taking the pill by giving four or five treats in rapid succession, with a hidden pill in one of them. If you can handle your dog's mouth, gently press the lips against the molars to open it. Drop the pill as far back on the tongue as possible. Close the dog's mouth, hold it shut, tilt the head upwards and gently massage the dog's neck to encourage swallowing. Some owners also talk or sing to the dog as an added distraction.*

minutes each day. Increased mobility will go a long way toward easing the stress and frustration that very often accompany this debility. At this stage of recovery the dog can also be fitted with a wheeled cart. Many dogs love the cart from the first time they try it. If your Dachshund is reluctant, try coaxing with treats or a *come* command.

When your Dachshund begins using the cart have safety measures in place such as ramps and door gates. It can be helpful to attach a bell to the cart. Some Dachshunds turn into two-wheeled devils zipping around the house or using their cart to intimidate other dogs.

For many dogs, training wheels are excellent rehab therapy; others must rely on them for life.

11

Complex Training and Behavior Issues

A few Dachshunds suffer from behavior issues that don't readily respond to straightforward retraining. Some of these include patterns established as a puppy and never effectively revised, inherent or hormonally triggered behaviors that were not addressed as they emerged, sociopathic behavior caused by deficient socialization, or neurologically based emotional instability or learning impairment. These problems are often present from an early age but don't become worrisome until adolescence. Professional consultation may be needed in order to fully understand their scope and devise the best means of resolving them.

Aggression

Aggression takes many forms ranging from dominant aggression directed toward familiar individuals and territorial aggression directed toward strangers to fear-based defensive aggression or predatory aggression. Warning signs usually precede an aggressive incident.

To determine the cause of your Dachshund's aggression analyze the factors leading up to the incident.

- Who was the intended target?
- Where did the incident occur?
- What was the dog's demeanor during the incident?

Dominant Aggression

Dogs use dominant aggression to protect valued possessions and improve their ranking in the family pack. In Dachshunds, this is most commonly due to opportunistic dominance. Associated behaviors emerge around 8–9 months and generally become problematic around 15–18 months, thanks to a combination of temperament, hormones, and human mismanagement.

Opportunism is part of the canine personality. A dog may develop perceptions of high rank if this idea is reinforced by human pack members. Minor victories, which often go unnoticed, encourage reliance on this approach in more situations. Triggers for aggressive outbursts

Training Tips

- *Dominant aggression is more common in males and neutering may help. In females, however, spaying may intensify the problem by raising testosterone levels. Neutering without concurrent behavior modification will not substantially revise learned opportunistic dominance.*
- *Basic obedience training will help reinforce your role as pack leader but your dog may not be permitted to join a group class until the problem is under control.*
- *A low-protein diet has been shown to help curb aggressive tendencies in some dogs.*
- *DAP- Dog Appeasing Pheromone (see page 118) may help diffuse anxiety*
- *In severe cases a veterinary behaviorist may prescribe medications to control aggressive behavior.*

or attention in response to the dog's demands or permit begging at the table. Simply being near food or in the kitchen during mealtime can activate aggression in some dogs. Furniture, especially the bed is also a common trouble spot. The dog should eat and sleep in a crate during remedial treatment.

Territorial Aggression

All dogs are instinctively territorial but territorial aggression is traceable to a combination of instinct and learning. Poorly socialized dogs are prime candidates for this problem. It is also a common behavior issue for dogs that are left outdoors unsupervised. Some Dachshunds tend to become obsessively interested in their home territory, making them more reactive toward anything unfamiliar. Others are aloof and suspicious, but don't possess a natural inclination to challenge intruders. This response may be inadvertently encouraged by praising the dog for protectiveness or permitting antisocial responses.

A territorial dog in defensive mode exhibits raised hackles, bared teeth, and a threatening low-pitched bark. This behavior is self-reinforcing and a dog in this highly focused and aroused state may bite if someone attempts to intervene. Puppies begin displaying territorial behavior such as defensive barking and intolerance of strangers when their socialization period ends at three or four months of age. This may evolve into territorial guarding during adolescence, but usually doesn't become a serious problem until adulthood.

Despite their reluctance, naturally wary Dachshunds should regularly visit unfamil-

like food, toys, or perceived social challenges are predictable, but some dogs become prone to random volatility, which increases the risk of being bitten. Directly confronting an aggressive dog is likely to intensify the behavior. Never assume that your own dog will not bite you.

The first step is to identify and avoid situations likely to provoke aggression such as approaching the dog while eating or attempting to take something away.

Toys, food, walks, or attention should be strictly controlled. Access to anything important should be preceded by compliance with a command to establish leadership. It may be necessary to keep the dog on a house leash to accomplish this. Adhere to a structured routine. Never provide food

Food is a common trigger for aggression.

iar locations. This helps to alleviate a budding obsession with home turf and balances out their sensitivity and reactivity to the environment. It won't help defuse aggression. Professional assistance may be needed to desensitize and counter-condition aggressive reactions.

Avoid situations likely to encourage aggression. Behavior modification involves slowly introducing the dog to potentially threatening situations to build tolerance. It is helpful to begin this training in a neutral location less likely to encourage a guarding instinct.

Predatory Aggression

Dachshunds exhibiting strong predatory drive must have early training to shape and control it. This includes socialization to other species, interactive play to teach bite control, and obedience training to instill a recall command. Otherwise, the dog may have no ability to control prey drive when it takes over.

This is the most difficult type of aggression to modify. It is highly pleasurable, which is obvious in the typical excited and happy body language associated with it. Predatory aggression is typically directed toward animals rather than humans, but any fast-moving individual can incite the urge to chase and bite.

Unlike a defensive bite that uses only the incisors, a prey bite uses the entire jaw and all the teeth to seize the target. This isn't the only possible danger. An out of control Dachshund is at constant risk of being hit by a car or attacked by larger dogs. Until the problem is managed, the dog must be confined in an escape-proof area and exercised on lead.

Unlike other forms of aggression, there is little likelihood that a dog in prey mode

This Dachshund is enjoying being introduced to a new environment and another species.

Dog-Appeasing Pheromone (DAP)

Pheromones, unique chemical compounds, are the most powerful form of canine communication. The messages contained in these unique scents are undetectable by humans but instantly recognizable by every dog. The ability to smell is a puppy's only well-developed sense at birth. The pheromone produced by lactating dams activates the bonding process by triggering a sense of security in newborns. Dogs of any age instinctively respond to this scent. A synthetic form has been developed as a calmative.

In clinical trials it has been shown useful to reduce tension leading to various undesirable behaviors. It is commercially available as an aerosol spray, a scent-impregnated collar, or an electric diffusing unit. Two weeks of constant exposure may be needed before effects are noted.

will turn on you. Leash corrections can help interrupt the prey sequence, and aversive therapy may be the only way to stop it. If you prefer to try counter-conditioning extensive work may be needed. If your Dachshund spots a potential target during a walk, encourage the dog to focus on you. Give the *look* command and provide a reward. Cultivating this ability to shift out of prey drive takes time. For some dogs, it must be continually reinforced. Desensitization may also work to raise the dog's response threshold to potential targets. It should always be done in controlled situations and may require a combination of reinforcement and corrections. Unlike stress-motivated aggression, predatory aggression is easily diffused through exhaustion. Much of it can be alleviated simply by ensuring that the dog gets plenty of exercise.

Defensive Aggression

Defensive aggression, a combination of instinct and learning, is motivated by self-protection. While some dogs freeze, run, or hide when they feel threatened, defensive aggressors resort to a combination of growling, snapping, whining, and cowering.

Signs of defensive aggression may begin to emerge by four or five months of age; a full-blown problem usually becomes evident at 18 to 24 months. It typically develops slowly as the dog becomes increasingly reliant on defensive aggression in response to challenging situations. Without treatment, a timid dog can develop more serious problems such as defensive aggression. Forcing the dog to confront anything that triggers extreme anxiety can lead to chronic anxiety or fear-based aggression. A major portion of misdirected aggression is a fear-based attempt to relieve anxiety.

Never reprimand a dog for fearful aggression and do not reinforce it through misdirected reassurance. Panic triggers a chemical reaction in the brain which makes cognitive thinking impossible. Realize that the dog is responding purely from instinct, and this sense of overwhelming fear is self-reinforcing. Revising the problem requires a combination of desensitization and counter-conditioning exercises. Desensitization exercises can help to develop tolerance for certain levels of stimulation. This may include reactivity to motion and noise or fear of strangers. In addition to defensive behavior this can trigger secondary coping behaviors to diffuse anxiety.

Most dogs can develop coping skills to manage their fears if they are given suffi-

Behavioral Pharmacology

In some cases, severe behavior issues fail to respond to therapy and medical intervention may be the only alternative. Possible physical causes should first be ruled out and drug therapy should be managed by a veterinary behaviorist.

Most of the commonly used medications are not FDA approved for this purpose and they are prescribed off label. Very few controlled studies have been conducted to determine optimal dosage regimes or document unexpected reactions to these drugs. Be aware of all potential risks, contraindications, and side effects known to be associated with them as well as the possible need for long-term or lifetime medication.

Gestures of Defensive Fear

- *Dilated pupils, avoiding eye contact, turning head away.*
- *Lip licking.*
- *Ears held back.*
- *Crouching posture.*
- *Tail down.*
- *Alternately barking, growling, and whining.*
- *Leaning backwards or slowly backing away from perceived threat.*

Coping skills are a combination of instinct and learned response.

Training Tip: Discouraging Predation
With your Dachshund on a 30-foot lead set up a situation to encourage chasing a target. When the dog nears the target it must be startled with a strong leash correction or a remote method such as a spray of water or a citronella collar or a frightening, but safe projectile. This therapy is time consuming. Repeated encounters must be set up and managed in a variety of situations, adding novel distractions to reinforce the message.

The socialization process must be tailored to a puppy's coping skills in order to prevent fears and phobias.

cient time and slow, positive introductions although longstanding problems may require professional advice.

Anxiety

Justified apprehension can be connected to specific situations or generalized due to lack of social skills or poor socialization. The response can be instinctive or learned, such as anxiety about visiting the veterinarian or groomer after a bad experience. One sufficiently traumatic encounter may be enough to instill a learned fear response triggered by any associated sight, sound, or smell. It can occur at any age, but most often surfaces during adolescence. Anxiety permits escape. Continually relying on this maladaptive behavior strategy leads to chronic stress.

Unchecked anxiety can grow as the dog increasingly anticipates real or imagined fears. Other common anxiety-driven behaviors in Dachshunds include obsessive territorial marking, or compulsive digging, chewing, or barking.

Anxiety Attacks
Learn to recognize the symptoms of anxiety in your pet.

Moderate Anxiety
- *Drooling or salivating*
- *Tail tucked*
- *Head lowered and eyes averted*
- *Trembling*
- *Ears held back*

Escalating Anxiety
- *Agitated pacing*
- *Panting*
- *Whining*
- *Hyperactivity*
- *Extreme vigilance*
- *Hyperventilating*

Training Tip: Don't Coddle

Every puppy's socialization includes a share of frightening experiences, but growing confidence, knowledge of the environment, and stress tolerance equip a puppy with tools to manage fear. Some puppies have difficulty getting past this point for a variety of reasons, but this problem can be corrected if it is addressed early. Be sensitive to your puppy's coping skills, but forge ahead with the socialization process. After your puppy is immunized, arrange short, positive introductory visits to places such as the vet's office, to offset the possibility of a fearful reaction when an actual vet exam takes place.

A bad experience can traumatize a puppy but inadequate social skills are a bigger handicap. New experiences should always be presented in a highly positive manner. Puppies instinctively look to their pack leader for reassurance, and you must impart the message that new things are interesting and harmless. Resist the urge to coddle. Overwhelming fear combined with an overprotective reaction can reinforce the puppy's fearful impression.

- Identify and remove causes known to trigger or intensify anxiety.
- Implement a structured routine to create a sense of security.
- Maintain a secure environment—anxious dogs may try to escape when panicked.
- Reinforce the *relax* command.
- Use counter-conditioning to interrupt and redirect anxiety-driven behaviors.

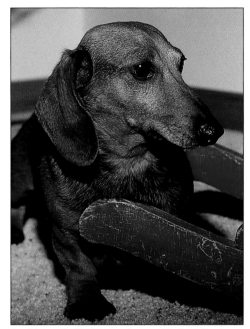

Avoidance behavior can become a chronic maladaptive response.

Fear and Avoidance

Some fears are instinctive; others develop as learned associations to specific triggers such as large dogs, vet exams, or car trips. By seven weeks, puppies have an excellent capacity to remember unpleasant experiences and avoidance responses can form quickly. A traumatic experience such as physical pain, harsh correction, or bullying by another pet can create a lasting avoidance response. A few bad experiences can set the pattern that may be difficult to overcome. However, learned fears can be replaced by new responses.

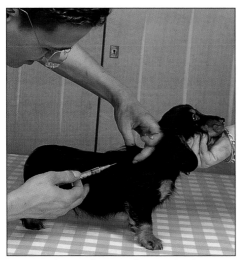

A traumatic experience at the veterinarian is a common cause of fearfulness.

Indications of Extreme Fear
- *Freezing*
- *Cowering*
- *Dilated pupils*
- *Whale eye (whites of eyes showing)*
- *Attempting to flee*
- *Sudden extreme shedding*
- *Involuntary urination*
- *Expressing anal sacs*

Wariness vs. Fearfulness

Natural wariness is a genetically controlled trait all dogs possess to some degree. It can be confused with shyness. Wary dogs are at ease within their pack, but exhibit suspicious reactions towards unfamiliar individuals despite comprehensive socialization. Many Dachshunds, like many dogs in general, are not overtly extroverted. They may be very sociable within their own familiar group, but not spontaneously welcoming to outsiders. While you may never turn this type of Dachshund into a social butterfly, inappropriate responses like chronic barking at strangers should be discouraged; otherwise these reactions may escalate. It may require ongoing work to prevent the dog from slipping back into former habits if counter-conditioning exercises are stopped.

Fear of Car Travel

Fears about cars or car trips may be a primary or a secondary reaction. Occasionally, the original fear becomes linked to other associations, such as motion sickness, fear of a particular destination, fear of unfamiliar surroundings, fear of crate confinement, or a lasting reaction to a traumatic incident. As a result, the dog displays extreme fear whenever a car trip is imminent and anything associated with that may trigger agitation. This makes it difficult to discover the true source of the problem.

In order to revise this problem you must instill positive associations about every aspect of the situation. Start small with five-minute sessions of placing the dog in a crate in the car, while providing treats, praise, or a toy for distraction. It may also be helpful to place an item of clothing with your scent in the crate. Some dogs feel more comfortable in an open wire crate. It may also help to leave the crate door open at first. DAP (see page 118) may also help combat anxiety. Reward all

Desensitization: Overcoming Fears of Unfamiliar People or Dogs

Maintain a log and note the consistent characteristics of situations that trigger fear. This will help you determine the parameters of your Dachshund's fear response.

How close do people or dogs approach before your dog becomes fearful?

Can the dog tolerate any amount of time in the presence of strangers or other dogs before anxiety commences?

1. Begin introductions in a safe, neutral location such as visiting a public place and observing strangers from a distance.
2. Encourage the dog to focus on something positive during these encounters. This is usually accomplished by constantly feeding treats as a distraction but experiment to see what works best for your dog. The "relax" command can be used to diffuse anxiety. Targeting can help redirect the dog's attention. A toy can be used to elicit prey drive and shift the dog's attention away from the source of fear.
3. Encourage the dog to explore and interact but never insist. Accepting attention from strangers or other dogs should always be voluntary.
4. Over the course of several weeks, increase your proximity to the potential fear as the dog's tolerance level increases. If the dog refuses to take treats or respond to you the stress threshold has been exceeded. Remove the dog from the situation and end the day's exercise.

Slow, positive interactions are needed to overcome fearfulness.

Desensitizing your dog to his or her fear of car travel can be a lengthy process.

efforts to remain calm. End the exercise as soon as the dog shows signs of agitation. The dog should begin tolerating being in the car in three to four weeks. This part of the exercise also helps you identify specific fear triggers such as the sound of car doors closing or the engine starting.

When your dog has reached a point of staying calm and responsive in the car begin adding short five-minute drives to the exercise. If necessary, have another person available to interact with the dog while you drive. As a precaution, the dog should always be crated while the car is moving and leashed before being let out of the car at an unfamiliar location.

When the dog is able to remain calm during the drive, add an enjoyable destination to the exercise. During each progressive phase of therapy continue gradual introductions, desensitization exercises, and regular evaluation to identify the specific basis of the fear.

Phobias

Most fears develop slowly and become progressively worse. Phobic reactions, in contrast, are characterized by sudden, uncontrollable levels of panic. Common triggers include thunderstorms, fireworks, or loud noises. These extreme reactions normally surface after one year of age, often in combination with other anxiety driven behaviors. Phobic reactions are suspected to have a genetic component but can also be triggered by a specific frightening incident.

Behavior modification techniques alone may have a limited effect on reversing the problem. These may include a combination of desensitization exercises, drug therapy, and carefully managing the dog's environment to minimize fear.

Separation Anxiety

Dachshunds behaving badly when unsupervised are not that uncommon. Most cases are due to a combination of poor training, boredom, and excess energy. True separation anxiety triggers a state of extreme distress when the dog is either left alone or separated from a particular person.

It can evolve into a generalized state of anxiety as the dog anticipates the dreaded event. Associated behaviors include whining, trembling, pacing, panting, and obsessively following you around the house before you leave. The dog may frantically avoid being crated or confined prior to your departure or try to escape from the premises after you leave. When left alone the dog may have lots of housetraining accidents, refuse to eat, or resort to chronic distress barking or destructive behavior like digging or chewing. The precise cause of separation anxiety is unknown. It is suspected to be a combination of generalized anxiety that is encouraged and reinforced by owner's responses. It is most common in rescue or shelter dogs under three years of age that are placed in a household with one owner.

Minimizing Separation Anxiety

- Provide plenty of exercise to ensure your dog is tired before you leave.
- Confine the dog to a safe, escape-proof area while you are gone. It may be

necessary to find a new location for this if the dog has already formed a negative association about confinement in this spot.

- Revise your departure routine and be careful to avoid giving the dog any cues that you are leaving. For instance don't jingle your keys or say goodbye, and leave at a slightly different time via another exit.
- Avoid effusive greetings when you return. Encourage your dog to remain as calm as possible.

Mild cases often respond to these steps in three to four weeks. If this doesn't result in any improvement, take a closer look at possible causes and reinforcements in the environment.

If the dog fears being left alone, a daycare program, dog walker, pet sitter, or getting another dog may solve the problem.

Treatment is more complicated if the dog dreads being separated from you. Use a combination of desensitization, counterconditioning, and relax exercises to teach stress tolerance and discourage obsessive attachment.

- Don't respond to attention-seeking behavior such as following you around the house.
- Help the dog to build tolerance for being alone. Begin with short periods of confinement while you are home. This allows you to monitor the dog's response and note how long an absence is tolerable before anxiety commences. Experiment to discover if radio, TV, chew toys, or DAP help maintain calmness. In some cases, it helps to give the dog a highly appealing treat

or chew toy right before you leave. This creates a positive association about your departure and helps to keep the dog occupied in your absence.

- Once you discover your Dachshund's tolerance level, you can use this as a starting point for counter-conditioning exercises. The goal is to keep the dog below the anxiety threshold during short periods of separation. Reward the dog for every calm response even if it's only a few minutes long.
- When your Dachshund becomes able to tolerate separation while you are home, begin adding random short absences. Avoid departure cues that are likely to trigger anxiety. If you return to a calm dog and a home that doesn't resemble a battlefield, you are making progress—but don't celebrate. The entire exit/entrance issue must be kept low key to avoid recurrence. Revising this behavior may take six to eight weeks.
- If your Dachshund does not respond to any of these measures within eight weeks, you may want to consider drug therapy.

Hyperactivity

If your Dachshund seems unable to calm down and continually pesters you for attention, hyperactivity may be the cause. Typical behaviors include barking, whining, pacing, obsessive licking or chewing, or chronic destructive behavior.

Many Dachshunds are energetic and most cases of hyperactivity are simply due to immaturity or a lack of appropriate outlets for mental and physical energy.

If this sort of behavior persists into adulthood and you are sure your dog has sufficient attention and exercise, there may be another reason. Hyperactivity can also be due to genetic predisposition or anxiety.

The first step is to ensure that the dog has adequate mental and physical stimulation. These needs can vary, and some Dachshunds have a surprisingly high need for daily activity.

Short, daily training sessions will also help the dog learn to focus and develop self-control. A structured routine provides reassurance that will help to reduce generalized anxiety. However, if there is a specific reason for this anxiety the source must be identified and dealt with as a separate issue.

Cognitive Dysfunction

Cognitive dysfunction is comparable to Alzheimer's disease both in cause and symptoms. This is a progressive degenerative behavior syndrome associated with brain aging. A buildup of plaque deposits in the brain, altering its neurochemical balance. The most pronounced symptoms are decreased responsiveness, impaired memory, and decreased learning ability. This leads to gradual disorientation such as confusion about normal routines, inability to recognize family members, or wandering off and becoming lost. Onset may begin as early as age seven. It has been diagnosed in one-quarter of dogs between the ages of 11–12; more than half of those over the age of 15 show some symptoms.

Symptoms of Cognitive Dysfunction

- Separation anxiety
- Unexplainable aggression toward humans or other dogs
- Housetraining lapses
- Compulsive barking or whining
- Nocturnal wandering
- Attention-seeking behavior
- Altered sleep patterns
- Deterioration of learning—forgetting basic commands and routines
- Loss of interest in surroundings, lessening desire to interact or engage in normal routines
- Aimless pacing or wandering

What You Can Do

Behavioral, medical, and drug therapies can be used to treat dogs with cognitive dysfunction.

Behavioral Therapy
- Provide regular walks, grooming sessions, and social interaction to encourage mental stimulation. In some cases, the dog should be treated as a young puppy, needing close supervision and frequent reinforcement.
- Encourage the dog to maintain a normal routine. This can also help alleviate housetraining lapses that often accompany cognitive dysfunction. Reluctance to go outdoors may be intensified by back pain, lameness, or failing eyesight. It may be necessary to provide an alternate exercise area or revise the dog's schedule to minimize exposure to envi-

A canine companion can be the answer to separation anxiety.

ronmental factors causing distress such as noise, commotion, or exposure to rambunctious pets.

■ Avoid stressful changes in the dog's environment. Older dogs are typically intolerant of change and this may cause the dog to become fearful, withdrawn, or unduly anxious. Associated symptoms can become especially pronounced if the dog is subjected to a combination of a disrupted schedule and new surroundings due to traveling, vacationing, or moving to a new home.

Drug Therapy

Antioxidant supplements, vitamins E and C, selenium, beta carotene, L-carnitine, lipoic acid, and omega-3 fatty acids have been shown to slow the progression of cognitive dysfunction in some cases. L-deprenyl (selegiline hydrochloride or Anipryl), an enzyme inhibitor, has also been successful in treating some cases.

Veterinary Behaviorists

Canine behaviorists specialize in evaluating serious behavior issues such as aggression or phobias. By analyzing the underlying motivations, they can offer techniques that will help to modify or manage problems or, at the very least, prevent them from getting worse.

Even though this is one of the fastest-growing specialties in veterinary medicine it remains an inexact science. The mechanisms that control behavior are not completely understood. Nor does extensive theoretical knowledge guarantee practical skill. Evaluating the qualifications of various practitioners can be confusing. Titles and job descriptions abound, and certification is not mandatory, everyone offering services of this type. A true animal behaviorist has a Ph.D. in applied animal behavior or board certification as a veterinary behaviorist. Behavior specialists, animal behaviorists, dog psychologists, or behavioral consultants may have some type of certification, but that in itself means nothing. They are not required to meet particular professional standards or licensing requirements.

If you feel that your Dachshund's problem warrants professional advice of this nature, your choice should be based on an individual's academic background, practical experience, and treatment recommendations. They should be forthcoming about the possible duration and costs of treatment and their success rate treating similar problems. You should feel comfortable with their techniques and confident in their abilities.

12 *Dachshund Sports*

Dog sports are fun, but that is just one reason why they are an important aspect of training. Teamwork strengthens the dog/owner bond and gives you new appreciation for what this breed is all about. It will also introduce you to facets of your Dachshund's personality of which you were previously unaware.

Evaluating Your Dachshund's Mental and Physical Aptitude for Sports

Dog sports are more than just fun and games. They require a big commitment and a good deal of common sense. Some sports like obedience and agility test a dog's mental skills and dexterity in a competitive arena. Others like earthdog and tracking tests measure natural aptitude and instinct in a non-competitive situation.

It is your responsibility to make sure that a particular sport and a training program is right for your Dachshund. Although you may enjoy it, your Dachshund may not be mentally or physically equipped for it.

Choosing the Right Instructor

Some Dachshunds also require a specialized approach to succeed. In that case you will have limited success without the help of an instructor able to recognize those needs and provide a training regime to address them.

Instructors at this level are less likely to have extensive background in behavior issues because behavior modification usually does not figure into advanced training programs. The dogs are expected to be capable of a certain level of training and a trainer may not recognize a dog's inability to cope with the routine. Continuing in the hopes that your dog will eventually calm down, figure things out, and get with the program can permanently undermine the training you have already accomplished with your dog.

Clear it with the Veterinarian

Health is just as important as mental aptitude. Have your Dachshund's eyes, hips, and elbows evaluated before you start training. No dog is perfect, but your Dachshund should be constructed well enough to tolerate athletic challenges. Minor structural faults that won't cause a problem under normal circumstances may not be able to handle athletic stress. The bones and joints of a dog's front assembly must support more than half of the total body weight. Shoulder, hip, and knee joints must be able to provide power and leverage and absorb the repeated shock of running and jumping. Weaknesses at either end will put additional stress on the muscles supporting your Dachshund's back, which can lead to back injuries. Many poor performances are due to lower back weakness or injury.

Make sure your dog's feet are in top condition. Soft footpads or weak foot tendons and overly long nails will reduce a dog's endurance and may lead to injuries.

Condition for Athletics

The goal of a conditioning program is to improve your dog's balance, coordination, and flexibility in order to minimize the possibility of athletic injuries. An unfit dog will be predisposed to muscle strains, soft tissue injuries, and lameness.

Treat your Dachshund like an athlete in training. Overweight dogs should slim down to their ideal weight before commencing any rigorous sport or exercise routine.

Your dog's conditioning program should be designed and managed just as carefully as his training program.

Pace the Routine to Your Dog's Abilities

Sports can definitely help puppies gain both confidence and self-control but training must be gauged to their growing aptitude. Puppies don't always have the strength, stamina, or concentration power for full participation and you must remain mindful of possible limitations.

Avoid strenuous roadwork to prevent excessive stress on growing bones and

Get your veterinarian's okay before starting your Dachshund on a sports program.

joints. Temperament also goes through some delicate growth stages that are liable to complicate training. Excitable, distracted puppy behavior is often replaced by willful unruliness during adolescence. Natural instincts also have a profound influence on training, making a hound more focused on predation and less mindful of social cues. Training and sports are valuable at any age, but you should accept the fact that your Dachshund may not settle down to accomplish any serious work until one or two years of age.

Is there a canine super athlete lurking within your Dachshund?

dog might overdo it, but creates a greater risk for injuries. Retrieving balls and frisbees and making sharp turns at high speeds account for the highest percentage of canine sports injuries.

Be aware of the particular strength and flexibility required for various sports. For instance, you may need to work on your dog's ability to push through heavy brush, squeeze into dark tunnels, or run long distances in varying weather.

Be aware of your dog's weaknesses. This not only allows you to focus the conditioning routine, it makes it easy for you to see when your dog is tired or sore. Videotaping is another great tool to help you assess your dog's performance and discover where more work is needed. It also gives you opportunities to analyze your performance, especially how it contributes to the dog's achievement level.

Conditioning for Sports

Comprehensive conditioning should include a range of activities to ensure that all muscles get a balanced work out. Alternate strength training and endurance-building routines to cultivate speed, stamina, resiliency, and drive.

This can be achieved with a combination of activities such as long walks and hiking, and hard running on flat terrain. Encourage the dog to run at a comfortable pace rather than to wildly tear around. This not only increases the risk that your

Warm Up, Cool Down

Wait at least two hours after mealtime before allowing your Dachshund to perform strenuous exercise. When starting a conditioning program it is important to provide plenty of water breaks to discourage the habit of gulping down an entire bowl of water at once. Some dogs also benefit from a high-energy snack during a strenuous workout.

Every session should start with a five-minute warm up. Massage your dog's hips and shoulders in a firm circular movement. For Dachshunds, back stretching is especially important. Encourage the dog to do plenty of back stretching and flexing. Run your fingertips along the dog's back from tail to neck, scratching up the coat against grain of hair. Follow up each session with cool-downs such as a short walk and a rubdown.

Most physical therapists advocate varied exercise routines and recommend giving the dog one day off every week. Many handlers also recommend switching to light training sessions for two days before a big event.

Managing Stress

Another important aspect of your conditioning program is helping your dog learn to cope with the mental stress of intensive training and competition. A Dachshund's intelligence creates ongoing training challenges. Every handler hopes for a perfect performance but if you overwork or over drill your Dachshund there is a great risk of losing the dog's attention and motivation. If your dog performs a flawless training routine, quit for the day. Do not force the dog to endlessly repeat it. Prolonged exposure to an unfulfilling activity is guaranteed to derail a Dachshund's performance motivation.

You must also recognize the difference between learning plateaus, boredom, and confusion. If the dog is bored, even a negative reaction from the handler may be perceived as a welcome change of pace. Dachshunds learn by trial and error, and decision-making requires a lot of effort. It's not that unusual for a dog to decide that doing nothing or running away is easier than the hard work of figuring out a training challenge. A huge range of internal and external factors continually influence your Dachshund's performance level and even successful training techniques require

When you enter the show ring, you are there to give a performance. Don't let your nerves get the better of you.

occasional adjustments to accommodate a dog's shifting response. Boredom, stress, hormonal changes, miscommunication, or frustration can all redirect motivation and it is your responsibility to use the right approach for your dog. Too much rigid correction will stifle drive and enthusiasm, too little will encourage sloppy work and mistakes. It's essential to keep your Dachshund thinking, rather than mindlessly obeying commands in order to prevent stress and frustration.

Competition inevitably induces stress and human stress invariably translates into canine stress. Dachshunds are proficient at reading and responding to human emotions and your disappointment will be impossible to conceal. You may need to step back and take another look at your attitude and goals before it has a negative impact on your dog's performance. This doesn't mean you should not set goals but keep them in perspective. Don't compare your Dachshund's performance to the accomplishments of other competitors working with different breeds. Nor should you set big expectations for your Dachshund during training or in the show ring. Your goals should pertain to yourself and factors within your control, like improving details of your performance and training routine.

Maintaining good communication with your dog is one of the most important things you can do in this respect. A major part of the training process involves teaching your dog to prioritize social interaction with you. It is much easier to train a dog to defer to a handler rather than to invest time and effort into effective communication, but this approach will never create a sustained level of enthusiasm. Under those conditions, it becomes more likely that your Dachshund will become bored, ignore you, or misunderstand you. It's also possible to get the right response from a dog for the wrong reason and that sort of training will not hold up in the long run. You want a fast, accurate response from your Dachshund, but no amount of drilling will create enthusiasm or motivation.

Competitive success is built on teamwork. Your Dachshund should perceive interactions with you as the best reward. Everything else should be secondary.

This becomes especially important when training for sports that do not have the built-in incentive of self-rewarding behavior. When you enter the show ring, you are there to give a performance. This is not the time or the place to work on training. If you are encouraged to enter your Dachshund in trials or tests before you are both prepared, your dog is going to make mistakes. You will not have the option of addressing this while you are in the ring and your dog will immediately discover that different rules apply in class than in the show ring.

Dachshunds require a considerable amount of feedback during training, but this is not permitted in all competitive situations. Training utilizes plenty of rewards and reinforcements but at some point, your Dachshund must be prepared to work without them. If reinforcements are cut back too abruptly or you have not sufficiently conditioned your dog to internalize the behavior, your training will fall apart. Your Dachshund may immediately begin sizing up more appealing alternative options or simply decide that the rules no longer apply. Dachshunds are far too smart to forget something like this once they have figured it out.

Before you enter the show ring, your Dachshund must be distraction-proof because the distractions at dog shows are countless. For instance, the breed's natural tendency to sniff an unusual environment will be instantly reinforced the first time your dog finds bait dropped by other handlers.

Obedience

While there are plenty of good reasons to try obedience as a sport, Dachshunds are not a breed traditionally viewed as top obedience competitors. Focus, responsiveness, and willingness are considered essential and these traits don't come naturally to every Dachshund. That doesn't imply that a Dachshund can't succeed at obedience, but you should be prepared for a challenge.

Many handlers emphasize the importance of choosing the right dog, but it is equally important to choose a partner that will complement your personality and working style.

The prospect of training a puppy is always exciting, but it can be a gamble for this reason. Many successful competitors recommend choosing an obedience Dachshund that is between one and two years of age in order to have a better idea of the dog's personality and training potential.

Some trainers also recommend the unorthodox approach of working backwards to train a Dachshund for obedience, starting with utility exercises. Much advanced work like scent discrimination, jumping, and retrieving, utilizes natural instinct and this can make it easier for a Dachshund to maintain motivation. This approach gives the dog opportunities to gain confidence and approval while building an internal reward mechanism to tackle more regimented work.

Whatever approach you use, remember that competitive obedience presents physical and psychological challenges that require insight and patience. Devote plenty of time to bonding with your dog. Work slowly and make sure your dog thoroughly understands each exercise before progressing to the next level.

AKC Events

Obedience Trial Champion (OCTH) is one of the most difficult AKC titles to obtain. First offered by AKC in 1977, a UD title is required in order to compete at this level. Dogs must earn 100 points and three first-place finishes under three different judges.

The Dachshund Club of America has held obedience trials in conjunction with its annual specialty show since 1961. The highest scoring dog at their first event was Han-Jo's Alexander, a longhair owned by Joseph and Hannelore Heller.

Rally

Rally became an official AKC event On January 1, 2005. It was originally meant to be an introductory step for beginning obedience competitors but it quickly surpassed the popularity of traditional obedience.

A rally course consists of 10–20 stations where handlers and dogs must stop to perform a specific obedience exercise. Each team begins with 100 points and deductions are made for errors. To earn a title the dog requires three qualifying scores of 70 or better from two different judges.

AKC offers three levels of titles in Rally Obedience. Rally Novice (RN), Rally Advanced (RA), and Rally Excellent (RAE).

Agility

Agility originated in England in 1978 and it became an official AKC event in 1994. Like obedience, it requires excellent communication between dog and handler. Because it's done off lead, basic obedience training is recommended for Dachshunds before commencing agility work.

Competitors must navigate an obstacle course of jumps, tunnels, weave poles,

Take things slow at first. Give your Dachshund plenty of time to learn the agility course.

dogs. Dachshunds compete in the 8–10 inch division or the 12–14 inch division.

There are three increasingly challenging levels of novice, open, and excellent courses. The obstacles are arranged a bit differently on every course and each level presents more complexity. Novice divisions contain approximately 12 obstacles, compared to advanced courses that may have up to 20. Advanced level courses also require covering more distance and navigating more obstacles at faster speeds.

To earn an agility title a dog must earn three qualifying scores of a minimum of 85 points out of a possible 100 within the specified time and fault limits.

Novice Agility (Divisions A and B)
12–13 obstacles
Open Agility for dogs that have Novice or Open titles
15–17 obstacles, including bar jumps and weave poles
Excellent Agility
18–20 obstacles

Additional AKC agility titles were added in 1998. Jumpers with Weaves classes include jumps, tunnels, and weave poles but no contact obstacles and the competition focuses solely on speed and jumping skill. Four levels of competition include novice, open, excellent, and master excellent. In 1999 the AKC also added the Master Agility Championship MACH.

AKC Agility Titles
Novice Agility (NA)
Open Agility (OA)
Agility Excellent (AX)
Master Agility Excellent (MX)

and contact equipment within a predetermined time limit. Timing is crucial to a successful performance and your dog relies on your verbal commands and body language while running a high-speed course with multiple obstacles. When you begin working your Dachshund in agility it's a good idea to start with lower versions of the obstacles for the first six months. This gives your dog an opportunity to develop needed strength, skill, and dexterity for quick turns and jumps.

The actual competition is separated into five size divisions based on the dog's height at the shoulders and certain aspects of the course are modified for smaller

Master Agility Excellent Preferred (MXP)
Master Agility Jumper (MXJ)
Master Excellent Jumper Preferred (MJP)
Preferred Agility Excellent (PAX)
Master Agility Champion (MACH)

In addition to AKC, Dachshunds can compete and earn agility titles in events sponsored by USDAA (United States Dog Agility Association), NADAC (North American Dog Agility Council), and CPE (Canine Performance Events).

Tracking

Tracking is fun and it provides terrific insight into how your Dachshund thinks. It's also a great way to give your dog a break from more structured forms of training. Dachshunds have a natural aptitude for several organized dog sports that are designed to test hunting instinct.

The breed is hardwired to follow a scent trail. Being low to the ground means that a Dachshund's nose is always close to the scent, but this is not their only physical advantage. The breed is physically designed to have the necessary body mass and natural leverage to easily follow trails through the thick brushy terrain and dense vegetation—spaces that would stop most dogs.

Although they have several natural advantages to do very well at tracking, some training is required. During a tracking test a dog must follow a stranger's scent trail and locate an article placed at the end. Dachshunds are naturally motivated to follow the scent of prey and they can be taught to follow a human trail with the same keenness. Excellent scenting ability is obviously required, but focus

> ### Tracking Facts
> The first Dachshund to earn a Tracking Dog Excellent title (TDX) was Cretel von Bupp Murr in 1980. The first Dachshund to earn a Variable Surface Tracking title (VST) was CT. DC Sadsack The Cupid Clone MW ME in 2002. MW denotes the miniature wirehaired variety, and ME signifies the AKC title of master earthdog.

and concentration are equally important in order to find and follow a trail without losing interest or becoming sidetracked. You cannot teach your Dachshund to track but instinct can be reinforced and refined through training. Like many other forms of training, the skills learned in tracking often prove to be equally useful in other areas, including other AKC events like field trialing, earthdog, and obedience competition.

AKC offers four tracking titles and each requires passing a non-competitive pass/fail test evaluated by two judges.

To earn a tracking dog (TD) title a dog must follow a scent trail in an open field 440–500 yards with three to five turns to locate a single scented article, typically a glove or wallet. The scent trail is fresh, laid within 30 minutes to two hours of the test. Two surveyor flags are placed to help the dog find the starting point and the direction of the track.

Dogs that have earned a TD title may go on to compete at the next level.

To earn a tracking dog excellent (TDX) title the dog faces additional challenges of a track that is three to five hours old,

Following a scent trail through the brush.

Earthdog

Like tracking tests, den trials were designed as an objective way to evaluate a dog's hunting instinct under natural working conditions. They were based on working trials originally devised in Germany and were first held in the U.S. in the early 1930s. At that time American breeders worried that Dachshunds were losing their natural working instinct and wanted a means to evaluate the Dachshund's primary function of routing vermin from underground dens. The test was designed to showcase the Dachshund's fearless temperament and willingness to enter a dark hole, squeeze along an underground tunnel, corner and hold the quarry at bay, and commence barking to signal the hunters where to dig. This requires a combination of mental and physical fitness. The dog must have strength, stamina, and leverage in order to slither over obstacles like rocks and roots without getting stuck.

For the test an artificial den is constructed from plywood and buried in a one-foot deep trench. A rat in a sturdy cage is placed at the end to serve as the quarry. In this situation the dogs work on instinct and very little training is required. However, it is not unusual for a dog to be overwhelmed or excited the first time around. Encourage your dog but don't worry if initial reactions range from aggression to distraction to fear. With repeated practice natural Dachshund instincts will emerge. Many handlers describe this as an instant transformation when the switch goes on in the dog's brain.

Some breeders begin training puppies for earthwork at seven or eight weeks of

approximately 800–1000 yards long with more turns and obstacles like roads, ditches, and diversionary tracks. The dog must locate four different articles on this track. Only one flag is placed at the start of the track and the dog is given no clues of the trail's direction.

The most challenging tracking test is variable surface tracking (VST), implemented by AKC in 1995; only 130 dogs have managed to earn this title in more than a decade. The dog must follow a scent trail covering many surfaces such as grass, sand, and concrete to locate four items made of four different materials: fabric, leather, plastic, and metal.

Passing both tracking dog excellent and variable surface-tracking tests qualifies a dog for the title of champion tracker.

age by encouraging them to explore a cardboard box with a small hole cut for the entrance. Place a treat inside and persuade the pup to enter. You can construct increasingly challenging cardboard tunnels as your pup's skill improves. When your pup is old enough to try the real thing, start with a short tunnel to make sure that the pup will not hesitate to enter a small dark enclosed space.

AKC began offering earthdog tests in 1994 based on a testing format designed by the American Working Terrier program. Earthdog tests are designed to gauge instinct, problem solving ability, determination, focus, and hunting instinct.

AKC earthdog tests are divided into four classes: introduction to quarry, junior earthdog, senior earthdog, and master earthdog. Dachshunds can earn three different titles by completing increasingly challenging tests, junior earthdog (JE), senior earthdog (SE), and master earthdog (ME).

Field Trials

According to the AKC's *Complete Dog Book,* field trials provide a "practical

During an earthdog test, a sturdy metal cage protects both prey and predator.

demonstration of a dog's ability to perform the functions for which it was bred." The first Dachshund field trial was held in the United States in 1935, in Lamington, NJ.

Dachshund field trials are competitive events where dogs are judged on their ability to trail a rabbit or hare. The goal is not to catch the rabbit but rather to demonstrate hunting instinct, desire,

Earthdog tests are designed to simulate the traditional Dachshund job of hunting badgers underground.

Dachshund field trial

perseverance, and the ability to accurately follow a trail.

Judges look for scenting and trailing ability, determination, endurance, adaptability, independence, courage, and hunting spirit.

Training Your Dachshund for Field Trials

Hunting instinct and working style is primarily instinctive, but training can help to refine it, direct it, and create the sustained motivation necessary for many hunting situations. Most Dachshunds will enthusiastically chase prey, but gusto must be combined with good sense and efficiency. Training provides guidance and structure to the natural learning process. This prevents a dog from developing unwanted habits like wandering off a difficult trail or getting into the habit of chasing quarry by sight. Field trial dogs are usually introduced to game between 6–12 months and it may

be difficult to motivate a dog that is introduced at a later age. You want your Dachshund to follow scent rather than to chase game by sight. All Dachshunds develop and learn at a different pace. Therefore hard and fast rules cannot be applied to development or training for field trials. Here are a few general suggestions.

■ Training should commence during a pup's socialization period between eight and sixteen weeks. At this age most pups willingly return to their handler rather than take off to pursue their own agenda. This becomes a bigger issue when prey drive strengthens during adolescence, but each pup should be worked individually to ensure a minimum amount of distractions.

■ Early training should include long walks in thickly wooded areas. Encourage the pup to investigate and become comfortable navigating through thick brush, while reinforcing the idea of paying attention and coming when called.

Your goal is for the dog to become an independent worker, able to figure things, but equally willing to take direction. The only AKC title offered in this sport for Dachshunds is a Field Championship. Dachshunds achieving conformation and field championships become dual champions.

Spurlaut

Trail barking, open trailing, or voicing is a valued, but not a mandatory trait for hunting and field trial dogs. AKC Field Trial rules were amended to designate it as desirable but it is not the only deciding factor in a competitive situation. Dachshund working tests given in Germany include a mandatory voice test. The dog is placed on a scent line and evaluated on the ability to follow a scent trail and bark.

Voicing has definite advantages in actual hunting situations. Open trailing makes it easy to keep track of a dog's location, gives a hunter valuable clues such as whether a trail is hot or cold. For example, when tracking a wounded deer, when a trail goes cold and scenting becomes difficult the dog may signal this by falling silent.

While most scent hounds are open trailers, many Dachshunds are not. Some have a natural tendency to do this, but many others trail silently. Like the hunting instinct, trail barking cannot be induced by training. In the 1930s, the researcher Leon Whitney confirmed that this behavior has a genetic basis. However, it does not easily respond to selective pressure. Some Dachshunds begin trail barking by the time they are five months old. Others

may not start until they reach one year of age. Seven months is considered to be the average age for this trait to emerge.

Dachshund Clubs

There are over 50 regional AKC member Dachshund clubs throughout the country. Most have monthly meetings, educational programs, training classes, and one or more organized events. They offer great opportunities to participate in Dachshund activities and meet other owners in your area.

DCA Versatility Certificate Program

Introducing your dog to multiple challenges is a great way to cultivate teamwork, sharpen your training skills, and discover hidden talents. Many Dachshund lovers do this without prompting because they recognize their dog's potential. The Dachshund Club of America (DCA) began taking an active role to encourage this in 1982, by implementing a versatility certification program. It provides special recognition for dogs that demonstrate skill in multiple areas. The program also aims to encourage fanciers to try out new activities and to keep breeders mindful of the Dachshund's heritage and versatility as a sport and hunting dog. Dachshunds are eligible to compete in six AKC events, more than any other recognized breed. Most Dachshunds are capable of a passable performance in at least three of these.

Dachshunds must demonstrate ability in at least three areas. They can earn

The Canine Good Citizen Program

The AKC's Canine Good Citizenship certification program was established to encourage and acknowledge the importance of polite, well-socialized dogs and responsible owners. To emphasize that goal, the title is offered to all dogs: purebred, mixed breed, registered, and unregistered. To qualify, a dog must pass a simple standardized test to demonstrate stable temperament and self-control. Canine Good Citizenship certification has now become a required qualification for a DCA versatility certificate and therapy dog certification. To find out about upcoming CGC tests in your area, visit the AKC Web site at www.akc.org.

The Dachshund Club of America (DCA)

The DCA is one of the country's oldest specialty dog clubs and remains dedicated to advancing the breed's heritage and celebrated versatility. To further that goal, the club offers a special award at their national specialty.

The DCA Triathlon program is designed to recognize the Dachshund's versatility by acknowledging accomplishments in field and performance events. DCA Triathlon medals are awarded to dogs entered in three to five events offered at the DCA national specialty: tracking, field trial, earthdog, obedience, rally, and agility.

points toward a versatility certificate in conformation, field, obedience, rally, tracking, agility, and earthwork. Versatility candidates must earn a Canine Good Citizenship title in addition to a total of 18 points in other sports. The point scale for various levels of accomplishment in each sport is determined by the DCA.

If you would like to try for a versatility certificate

1. Begin with a basic obedience course
2. Complete the requirements for an AKC Canine Good Citizen title.
3. Take classes and attend events to learn more about these various sports. Joining a local Dachshund club is a good way to meet experienced competitors and find out about upcoming events
4. When you decide on the sports you would like to try, don't go overboard. At first, it will require some intensive training to familiarize a dog with the basics of a new activity. Once that is accomplished, limit training for each sport to once or twice a week. Obsessive training completely defeats the purpose of encouraging a broad, adaptable range of skills. Keep in mind that dogs are not required to earn titles in each sport to qualify for a versatility certificate. For instance, Dachshunds can earn between three and ten points by participating in AKC conformation events to satisfy this requirement.

The test consists of a series of short, simple exercises. Although there are slight variations in the format, a typical Canine Good Citizenship test evaluates a dog's reactions in the following exercises, which are designed to mimic real life situations.

- React calmly as a friendly stranger approaches
- Sit quietly and tolerate attention from a stranger
- Accept being touched, groomed, or examined by a stranger
- Walk on a loose lead in a heel position
- Behave calmly when walking through a crowd
- Remain in a sit or down position on command
- Remain calm and collected when praised
- Behave politely in the presence of other dogs
- Act calmly in response to a surprising but non-threatening event such as opening an umbrella
- Remain capable of polite behavior when not supervised by owner

Sensitive and affectionate, Dachshunds can be well suited to therapy work.

Therapy Work

We don't need a research study to tell us that cuddling with a dog is great therapy. Our dogs instinctively realize when we are ill or upset, and they know exactly what to do to make us feel better. If your Dachshund seems to have the knack for this you may want to consider sharing this wonderful talent through therapy work.

The Delta Society, a non-profit group founded in 1977, was the first organization to investigate the idea of using dogs in a therapeutic capacity. They sponsored some of the earliest investigations to scientifically document the healing benefits derived from contact with animals. Their goal was to prove that regular contact with a pet enhanced a person's motivation to get well, aided the ability to cope with stress and anxiety, and helped to control panic attacks and depression.

Much to their surprise the research revealed much more. Interacting with a pet also provided measurable physical benefits, including lowering blood pressure and cholesterol levels, and controlling the release of various hormones into the bloodstream to create a sense of well being and minimize stress.

This research led to the formation of groups like Delta Pet Partners, dedicated to making these benefits available on a wide scale to patients in hospitals, nursing homes, and rehabilitation centers. Today, more than 8500 therapy dogs comfort and cheer more than a million people each year.

Small to medium-sized dogs, with a calm, affectionate temperament make the best candidates. A therapy dog doesn't need to be an obedience expert, but should have good self-control and reliably respond to basic commands. A well-trained Dachshund is an ideal candidate.

The actual work is not complicated. Many patients are immeasurably cheered simply by seeing an adorable four-footed visitor. Normally, the dogs are cuddled, petted, groomed, or walked. In order to become certified for therapy work a dog must undergo basic obedience training and earn an AKC Canine Good Citizen title. Dogs and handlers must also participate in a standardized training and evaluation program conducted by local chapters of a canine therapy group such as the Delta Society Pet Partners Program.

Hunting

In Germany, Dachshunds are required to successfully compete at working trials before earning a conformation championship. Aptitude for hunting Dachshunds can be demonstrated through 11 different tests—including hunting fox, badger, or rabbit, following a trail of wounded game, or finding game in underbrush—testifying to their versatility as hunters.

Field trials evaluate hunting aptitude but, in reality, there is no comparison between a competition and actual hunting experience. Dachshunds are among the world's most versatile hunting breeds. They can work above- and underground, alone, with another dog, or a pack. In addition to their unparalleled ability to hunt small game Dachshunds also excel at tracking large game or following the blood trail of wounded game. They can

Tracking Collars

A tracking collar can help to pinpoint a lost dog's location. The collar is fitted with a battery-operated transmitter that weighs about four ounces. It is linked to a handheld radio receiver and antenna that picks up radio signal from collar's transmitter.

A similar type of transmitter collar is also available to keep track of Dachshunds underground. The battery-operated transmitter emits a signal up to 15 feet. However, electric fences or buried electric cables can interfere with the signal's transmission.

Beeper collars can also help track a Dachshund in the field or locate a dog's whereabouts in thick cover. The collar will beep more frequently when the dog is stationary, which indicates when the dog is on the move.

be excellent for upland game work paired with a larger pointing or retrieving breed.

A Dachshund must have strong natural aptitude for this work. A great hunting dog is produced from a combination of intelligence, talent, instinct, and training.

But hunting requires more than energy and instinct. A dog that is highly motivated for field trialing may prove worthless in a real hunting situation; running off or becoming exhausted before accomplishing anything. A hunting dog needs courage, caution, intelligence, adaptability, and the ability to analyze each situation as it occurs. Some Dachshunds begin to show natural hunting aptitude by 10–12 weeks; others may not exhibit strong interest until

Dog sports are fun, and the teamwork required strengthens the bond between dog and owner.

they near adolescence. The age when this drive emerges has no bearing on a dog's eventual ability in the field. You should begin field training your puppy at five or six months. At this age the goal is to encourage natural prey drive, give the pup experience with game, and practice moving through brush. This is known as becoming *brush wise*. During all these activities practice giving your pup *recall* and *pay attention* commands until it becomes second nature.

Your goal is to have a dog that is responsive and stays within sight. In addition to the possibility of losing a roaming dog, a Dachshund that is in the habit of running off can be accidentally shot by a hunter. If you have problems keeping track of your Dachshund while hunting, it may help to have the dog wear a bell as a safety measure.

No training tool can be a substitute for the communication and cooperation that comes from training and teamwork. Hunt-

ing is a cooperative effort so prey drive must be balanced by social drive. When you are hunting with your Dachshund you should work as a pack in pursuit of a common goal. At this level the entire concept of giving or obeying commands becomes immaterial. You must be on the same wavelength.

Good Sports

Dog sports can be a fun, rewarding, and positive experience for both you and your Dachshund. You'll learn more than you dreamed about the breed's inherent characteristics and the temperament and personality of your dog. It takes hard work and commitment to create a successful human/dog team, but the resulting satisfaction is well worth it. Stay balanced, keep things in perspective, and remember that training and competition should be fun for both you and your dog.

Useful Addresses, Web Sites, and Literature

Books

Coppinger, Raymond & Lorna. *Dogs: A Startling New Understanding of Canine Origin, Behavior, and Evolution.* Scribner, 2001.

Donaldson, Jean. *The Culture Clash: A Revolutionary New Way of Understanding the Relationship Between Humans and Domestic Dogs.* James & Kenneth, 1997.

Dunbar, Ian. *How To Teach A New Dog Old Tricks.* James & Kenneth, 1998.

Falconer-Douglas. *Contemporary Dachshund, World Of Dogs.* TFH Publications, 1999.

Gordon, Ann. *Dachshund, Your Healthy Happy Pet,* 2nd Edition. Howell Book House, 2005.

McConnell, Patricia. *The Other End of the Leash.* Ballantine, 2002.

McLennan, Bardi. *Dogs and Kids.* Howell, 1993.

Pinney, Chris. *Dachshund*s. Barron's Educational Series, 2000.

Serpell, James. *The Domestic Dog, Its Evolution, Behavior and Interactions with People.* Cambridge University Press, 1995.

Stern, G.B. *The Ugly Dachshund.* J.N. Townsend Publishing, 1998.

Walker, Joan Hustace. *The Everything Dachshund Book,* Adams Media Corp., 2005.

Quirky, charming, and endlessly fascinating, Dachshunds live up to their well-earned reputation.

Periodicals

The Dachshund Review
Hoflin Publishing, Inc.
4401 Zephyr Street
Wheat Ridge, CO 80033
(303) 934-5656

The Miniature Dachshund Digest
5340 TR 187
Marengo, OH 43334
(419) 253-2406

Web Sites

Training and Behavior

American College of Veterinary
Behaviorists
www.animalbehavior.org

Animal Behavior Society
www.veterinarybehaviorists.org

International Association of Animal
Behavior Consultants
www.iaabc.org

American College of Veterinary
Behaviorists
www.veterinarybehaviorists.org

American Pet Dog Trainers
www.apdt.com

Karen Pryor Clicker Training
www.clickertraining.com

Health

Institute for Genetic Disease Control
www.vetmed.ucdavis.edu/gdc/gdc.html

American Animal Hospital Association
www.healthypet.com

Merck Veterinary Manual
www.merckvetmanual.com

Orthopedic Foundation for Animals (OFA)
www.offa.org

Sporting Activities

Agility

North American Agility Dog Council
11522 S. Highway 3
Cataldo, ID 83810
www.nadac.com

United States Dog Agility Association
P.O. Box 850955
Richardson, TX 75085
(972) 487-2200
www.usdaa.com

Agility Ability
www.agilityability.com

Earthdog

American Working Terrier Association
www.dirt-dog.com

American Kennel Club
www.akc.org/events/earthdog/info.cfm

Dachshund training is a working partnership built on respect and understanding.

Field Trials

American Kennel Club
*www.akc.org/events/field_trials/dachshunds/
index.cfm*

Hunting

*http://www.teckelclub.org/hunting-with-
dachs.htm*

Tracking

*http://www.akc.org/events/tracking/
index.cfm*

Obedience

http://www.akc.org/events/obedience/
*http://www.akc.org/events/obedience/
training_clubs/*

General Information

www.dog-play.com
www.workingdogweb.com

Therapy

Delta Society Pet Partners Program
www.deltasociety.org
info@deltasociety.org

Therapy Dogs International
www.tdi-dog.org
tdi@gti.net

Therapy Dogs Incorporated
www.therapydogs.com
therapydog@sisna.com

The Bright and Beautiful Therapy Dogs, Inc.
www.golden-dogs.org
info@golden-dogs.org

National Breed Rescues

Dachshund Club of America Rescue
3040 Old Darlington Road
Beaver Falls, PA 15010
(724) 846-6745

Almost Home Dachshund Rescue Services
36 Lincoln Laurel Road
Frelinghuysen, NJ 07825

Coast to Coast Dachshund Rescue
2292 Evelyn Avenue
Memphis, TN 38104

Organizations

American Kennel Club
5580 Centerview Drive, Suite 200
Raleigh, NC 27606
(919) 233-9767
www.akc.org

United Kennel Club
100 East Kilgore Road
Kalamazoo, MI 49001
(616) 343-9020
www.ukcdogs.com

Canadian Kennel Club
89 Skyway Avenue, Suite 100
Etobickie, Ontario
Canada M9W 6R4
(416) 675-5511
www.ckc.ca/en/

Dachshund Clubs

Dachshund Meet-up Groups
http://dachshund.meetup.com

The Dachshund Club of America
www.dachshund-dca.org

The National Miniature Dachshund Club
www.dachshund-nmdc.org

Your Dachshund's potential may surprise you.

Index

Wistful, contemplative, calculating—you never know what's going through a Dachshund's mind.

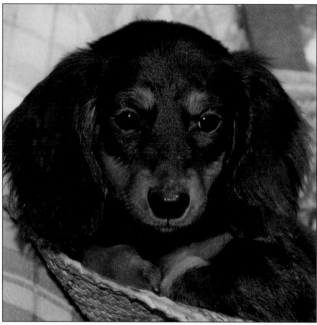

Dachshunds take their virtues for granted; training will give you a chance to appreciate them.